Stop Faking It!

Finally Understanding Science   So You Can Teach It

AIR, WATER, & WEATHER

Stop Faking It!

Finally Understanding Science   So You Can Teach It

AIR, WATER, & WEATHER

NSTApress

NATIONAL SCIENCE TEACHERS ASSOCIATION

Arlington, Virginia

NATIONAL SCIENCE TEACHERS ASSOCIATION

Claire Reinberg, Director
Judy Cusick, Senior Editor
J. Andrew Cocke, Associate Editor
Betty Smith, Associate Editor
Robin Allan, Book Acquisitions Coordinator

ART AND DESIGN David Serota, Director
PRINTING AND PRODUCTION Catherine Lorrain-Hale, Director
    Nguyet Tran, Assistant Production Manager
    Jack Parker, Electronic Prepress Technician

NATIONAL SCIENCE TEACHERS ASSOCIATION
Gerald F. Wheeler, Executive Director
David Beacom, Publisher

Library of Congress Cataloging-in-Publication Data

Robertson, William C.
  Air, water, and weather / by William C. Robertson.
      p. cm. — (Stop faking it! : finally understanding science so you can teach it)
  Includes index.
  ISBN 0-87355-238-5
  1. Weather—Study and teaching—Popular works. 2. Science—Study and teaching—Popular
works. 3. Science—Methodology—Popular works. I. Title.
  QC981.2.R63 2005
  551.6'071—dc22
                         2005003491

SC*i*LINKS. *Featuring sciLINKS®—a new way of connecting text and the Internet. Up-to-the-minute online
content, classroom ideas, and other materials are just a click away. Go to page xii to learn more about this new
educational resource.*

Contents

Preface vii

The Scope of This Book.. X

Everyday Items Used in Activities in This Book Xi

SciLinks Xii

Chapter 1   Under Pressure 1

Chapter 2   It's a Gas, Gas, Yeah..17

Chapter 3   Balloons and Other Things That Sometimes Float........ 39

Chapter 4   A Few Loose Ends 57

Chapter 5   Small-Scale Weather 69

Chapter 6   Large-Scale Weather 87

Chapter 7   The Severe Stuff 107

Glossary 117

Index 123

Preface

The book you have in your hands is the sixth in the *Stop Faking It!* series. The previous five books have been well received, mainly because they stick to the principles outlined below. All across the country, teachers, parents, and home-schoolers are faced with helping other people understand subjects—science and math—that they don't really understand themselves. When I speak of understanding, I'm not talking about what rules and formulas to apply when, but rather knowing the meaning behind all the rules, formulas, and procedures. I *know* that it is possible for science and math to make sense at a *deep level*—deep enough that you can teach it to others with confidence and comfort.

Why do science and math have such a bad reputation as being so difficult? What makes them so difficult to understand? Well, my contention is that science and math are *not* difficult to understand. It's just that from kindergarten through graduate school, we present the material *way* too fast and at too abstract a level. To truly understand science and math, you need *time* to wrap your mind around the concepts. However, very little science and math instruction allows that necessary time. Unless you have the knack for understanding abstract ideas in a quick presentation, you can quickly fall behind as the material flies over your head. Unfortunately, the solution many people use to keep from falling behind is to *memorize* the material. Memorizing your way through the material is a surefire way to feel uncomfortable when it comes time to teach the material to others. You have a difficult time answering questions that aren't stated explicitly in the textbook, you feel inadequate, and let's face it—it just isn't any fun!

So, how do you go about *understanding* science and math? You could pick up a high school or college science textbook and do your best to plow through the ideas, but that can get discouraging quickly. You could plunk down a few bucks and take an introductory college course, but you might be smack in the middle of a too-much-material-too-fast situation. Elementary and middle school textbooks generally include brief explanations of the concepts, but the emphasis is definitely on the word *brief*, and the number of errors in those explanations is higher than it should be. Finally, you can pick up one or fifty "resource" books that contain many cool classroom activities but also include too brief, sometimes incorrect, and vocabulary-laden explanations.

Given the above situation, I decided to write a series of books that would solve many of these problems. Each book covers a relatively small area of science, and the presentation is unrushed and hopefully funny in at least a few places. Typically, I spend a chapter or two covering material that might take up a paragraph or a page in a standard science book. My hope is that people will take it slow and digest, rather than memorize, the material.

This sixth book in the series is about air, water, and weather. It explores the physical science concepts associated with the behavior of air, water, and other fluids (yes, air can be considered a fluid!) and then uses weather as an interesting application of those concepts. As such, you will not find this to be a comprehensive book on weather. Of course, I do hope that the understanding you might gain from this book will help you immensely when you encounter other resources relating to weather concepts. After all, physical science concepts are at the heart of most weather concepts.

There is an established method for helping people learn concepts, and that method is known as the learning cycle. Basically, it consists of having someone do a hands-on activity or two, or even just think about various questions or situations, followed by explanations based on those activities. By connecting new concepts to existing ideas, activities, or experiences, people tend to develop understanding rather than rely on memorization. Each chapter in this book, then, is broken up into two kinds of sections. One section is titled, "Things to do before you read the science stuff," and the other is titled, "The science stuff." If you actually do the things I ask you to do prior to reading the science, I guarantee you'll have a more satisfying experience and a better chance of grasping the material.

It is important that you realize the book you have in your hands is *not* a textbook. It is, however, designed to help you "get" science at a level you never thought possible, and also to bring you to the point where tackling more traditional science resources won't be a terrifying, lump-in-your-throat, I-don't-think-I'll-survive experience.

Dedication

I dedicate this book to my mother, Arletta McIsaac, for her emotional, financial, and all other kinds of support that led me to this point. I also dedicate it to Donald McIsaac who, after the death of my father and in his infinite wisdom, became my stepfather and helped make two families even closer than they already were.

About the Author

As the author of NSTA Press's *Stop Faking It!* series, Bill Robertson believes science can be both accessible and fun—if it's presented so that people can readily understand it. Robertson is a science education writer, reviews and edits science materials, and frequently conducts inservice teacher workshops as well as seminars at NSTA conventions. He has also taught college physics and developed K–12 science curricula, teacher materials, and award-winning science kits. He earned a master's degree in physics from the University of Illinois and a PhD in science education from the University of Colorado. You can contact him at *wrobert9@ix.netcom.com.*

About the Illustrator

The soon-to-be-out-of-debt humorous illustrator Brian Diskin grew up outside of Chicago. He graduated from Northern Illinois University with a degree in commercial illustration, after which he taught himself cartooning. His art has appeared in many books, including *The Golfer's Personal Trainer* and *5 Lines: Limericks on Ice.* You can also find his art in newspapers, on greeting cards, on T-shirts, and on refrigerators. At any given time he can be found teaching watercolors and cartooning, or working on his ever-expanding series of *Stop Faking It!* books. You can view his work at *www.briandiskin.com.*

About the Cover

You probably recognize the character on the left as your basic loony weather forecaster, but you might be wondering who those other two guys are. The one blowing through the tent is supposed to be Daniel Bernoulli, a mathematician and physicist who studied, among many other things, air flow and air pressure. After you get through Chapter 2 in the book, you'll understand why he's blowing through a paper tent. The other dude is supposed to be Archimedes, who also studied math and physics, but did so much earlier than Bernoulli. He formulated a principle that explained buoyancy, which you'll read about in Chapter 3. Legend is he figured out buoyancy while trying to determine whether an object (a crown) was truly made of gold. He did so in his bathtub and then supposedly went around shouting, "Eureka!" Translation—"I have found it!" Not sure if that story is true. Anyway, the whole point of this cover drawing is to illustrate that a knowledge of the properties and behavior of air and water can serve as the basis for understanding a whole lot about weather.

The Scope of This Book

Many people will probably look at the last word in the title and assume that this is primarily a book about weather. They might also assume that my discussion of the properties of air and water will serve only as a prelude to understanding weather. Well, not so. I will deal with a number of concepts related to air and water that have little or nothing to do with weather. The reason for that is that some of these concepts are part of most science curricula even though they don't relate to weather. If I exclude them, I'm letting you down a bit, I think.

On the other hand, my treatment of weather in this book is not comprehensive. I pretty much limit myself to weather concepts that are good applications of the physics of air and water, and ignore those that aren't. For example, I don't discuss lightning, damage due to hurricanes, the scale used for measuring winds, or cloud types. Fortunately for you, there are lots of books in existence that cover these topics adequately. No sense in me redoing what's done well elsewhere.

So, this is not a book that covers every single property of air and water, nor is it a comprehensive book on weather. It's a book that combines portions of each of those topics, and, hopefully, helps you gain a basic understanding of enough concepts that you can do a better job teaching in all three areas.

Everyday Items Used in Activities in This Book

- Fork
- Flat-head nail
- Coffee can
- Duct tape
- Two empty soda cans
- Plastic straws
- Shallow pan
- Kitchen tongs
- One meter of rubber tubing (Tygon or other)*
- One bucket or saucepan of water
- Plastic water bottle
- Round balloons
- Votive candle
- One pickle jar or jar of similar size
- Index card
- Funnel
- Ping-Pong ball
- Small resealable plastic bags, 3cm × 5cm*
- Paper clips
- Slotted craft sticks*
- Vegetable oil
- Rubbing alcohol
- Clear drinking glasses
- Food coloring

- One cork
- One small, one medium Styrofoam ball*
- Modeling clay*
- Small rock
- Metal washers (equal size and weight)
- Several empty 2-liter soda bottles
- Pepper
- Two Cheerios
- Incense or other harmless producer of smoke
- One tornado tube or short section of foam pipe insulation
- Eyedropper
- Wooden matches
- Flashlight
- Pencil
- Pliers
- One empty toilet paper tube
- Two pushpins
- One emery board
- One human hair
- One table lamp without lampshade
- One sharp pencil
- One clear baking pan
- One section of cardboard

*Available from your local hobby shop or craft store.

How can you avoid searching hundreds of science websites to locate the best sources of information on a given topic? SciLinks, created and maintained by the National Science Teachers Association (NSTA), has the answer.

In a SciLinked text, such as this one, you'll find a logo and keyword near a concept, a URL (*www.scilinks.org*), and a keyword code. Simply go to the SciLinks website, type in the code, and receive an annotated listing of as many as 15 web pages—all of which have gone through an extensive review process conducted by a team of science educators. SciLinks is your best source of pertinent, trust-worthy internet links on subjects from astronomy to zoology.

Need more information? Take a tour—*www.scilinks.org/tour/*

Under Pressure[1]

The first thing I ought to address is why this book combines air, water, and weather. I addressed that in a preceding page, but it's worth another comment. In a regular physics textbook you'll find chapters on air and water and how they behave, and you can certainly find lots of books about weather. The reason I combine them here is that once you know a lot about air and other **gases**—and water and other **liquids**—you have many of the basics from which to understand weather patterns, what causes them, and how you can predict the weather. Of course, the air and water stuff is pretty interesting all by itself. If I didn't think that, I wouldn't waste your time and I'd spend my time more profitably, such as delivering pizzas.

"Pressure!! You want of know what pressure is?!! Air molecules trapped in a rigid container heated up to 212 degrees Fahrenheit. Unable to escape and moving faster than you can blink. That's pressure!!"

---

[1] I have no idea what your tastes in music might be, but if a David Bowie song comes to mind as you read this chapter heading, we're on the same wavelength.

I'm sure you are well aware of the distinction between solids, liquids, and gases, which might make you think that I'd treat air and water as very different things. Turns out, though, that as far as scientists are concerned, liquids and gases behave so much alike that we treat them just about as the same kind of thing— **fluids**. So, much of what we cover here will apply to both air and water. Those two things aren't exactly alike though, so we'll take different approaches from time to time. Do expect, however, that I'll be jumping around between the behavior of air and other gases, and water and other liquids—all the while pointing out where the two are similar and where they're different.

On to the contents of this chapter: We're going to deal with **air pressure** and water pressure and what causes those things to increase and decrease. We'll also deal with the real-world results of those increases and decreases in air and water pressure.

Things to do before you read the science stuff

Get a metal fork. Push on the palm of one of your hands with one tine of the fork (Figure 1.1). Don't do this so hard that you draw blood, but it should hurt just a bit. Now turn the fork around and push on the palm of your hand with the non-business end of the fork. Try to push just as hard as you did with the single tine, and compare the level of pain you get with the single tine and the non-stabbing end of the fork.

Figure 1.1

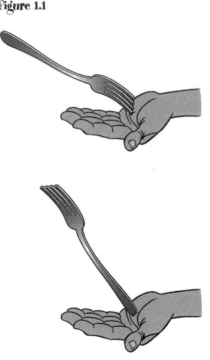

Here's something potentially more painful but maybe easier to get the point across. Get a flat-head nail, one of those that's pointed on one end (wouldn't be much of a nail if one end weren't pointed) and a completely flat surface on the other end. Push on the palm of your hand first with the pointed end and then with the flat end. Try to use an equal push each time and please, please, don't draw blood with the pointed end. Best to avoid poking yourself with nails unless you enjoy getting tetanus boosters.[2] Compare the level of pain with the pointed end and with the flat end.

---

[2] This is probably a good time to emphasize that this is a book for adults, and not a collection of activities for use in the classroom. Yes, you can adapt most of these activities for classroom use, but take care when doing so. For example, you probably don't want to turn a bunch of kids loose after telling them to poke themselves with forks.

The science stuff

Assuming you did as I told you and didn't end up in the ER, you should have noticed something. Even though you pushed *equally hard* with flat ends and sharp ends of things, the sharp ends hurt more. If you pushed equally hard, then that meant you pushed with the same **force** each time.[3]

Okay, if you pushed with the same force each time, why didn't it hurt the same amount each time? The answer has to do with how widely distributed that force was each time. When you pushed with the pointed end of the nail, the force was distributed over a very tiny area, and when you pushed with the flat end of the nail, the force was distributed over a much larger area. To take this to the extreme, suppose someone smashed his or her elbow into you with a force of about 100 pounds.[4] That would definitely hurt and leave a mighty bruise, and to be clear, I'm not recommending you have it done. Now suppose someone smashes a steel spike into you with a force of 100 pounds (apologies for the violence in this chapter so far!). That wouldn't just hurt, but would rather do serious damage or even kill you.

Now that I've made my point, here's a concept that helps you take into consideration not just how big a force one might exert, but the amount of area over which that force is spread. That concept is called **pressure**, and pressure is defined by

$$pressure = \frac{force}{area}$$

In case your math is a wee bit rusty, that line on the right means "divided by." Because force is in the numerator of that fraction on the right, a larger force means a larger pressure, and a smaller force means a smaller pressure. The area, however, is in the denominator. So, a larger area means a smaller pressure (the force is more spread out so the pressure is smaller) and a smaller area means a larger pressure (the force is more localized, so the pressure is larger).

SCI **L**INKS
THE WORLD'S A CLICK AWAY

Topic: pressure

Go to: *www.scilinks.org*

Code: SFAWW01

---

[3] First shameless promotion for one of the other books in this series, *Force and Motion: Stop Faking It! Finally Understanding Science So You Can Teach It*. I'm not going to pretend that you can't find out what the term *force* means by looking somewhere else than the dictionary, but if you want the thorough treatment, well, ...

---

[4] Using English units (pounds) instead of *Système International* units (which would be newtons for force) is a big no-no in science books, but I figure it's okay just this once given that most people have a good idea of how big a force 100 pounds is and very little idea how big a force 100 newtons is. For the record, a force of 100 pounds is equal to a force of 445 newtons.

Before moving on, I should tell you why pressure is such an important concept in dealing with air and water. The reason is that we're dealing with large numbers of atoms or molecules, and we tend to be concerned about the collective effect of all those atoms or molecules pushing on something. Having to worry about the individual forces exerted by millions upon millions of tiny particles is a royal pain, so we use the concept of pressure that describes their cumulative effect without dealing with individual forces.

More things to do before you read more science stuff

What I want you to do in this section are things you've probably already done, so maybe all you need is a good memory. If you haven't done these things, you'll get to take a field trip, so be sure to have your parents sign that permission slip.

Your first task is to undergo a reasonably large change in altitude. You can do this by taking a ride in your car in the mountains so you change altitude at least 500 feet (easy if you live where I do in Colorado and a difficult task in other areas), taking off and landing in a plane (expensive field trip!), or finding a tall building and riding the elevator up and down at least 20 floors. If you choose the last option, try to find an express elevator that isn't likely to stop every few floors. You'll get the effect better if you travel all the floors without stopping. If the elevator is in a fancy hotel, and it's prom night, you can probably find several teenagers to join you on the ride.

As you do any one of those tasks, or remember what it was like the last time you did, focus on the effect on your ears. Depending on whether you go up or down in altitude, and how far you have gone up or down, your ears will feel stopped up or they'll "pop" at some point. Some people can actually tell the difference in the feeling in their ears depending on whether they're going up or down in altitude, but to me it feels pretty much the same.

Okay, your next field trip is to a bathtub or a swimming pool. The swimming pool is a better option, but the bathtub (filled with water) will do. Basically, repeat your "change in altitude" procedure on a small scale. Move your submerged ears from one depth to another and notice changes in feeling in your ear. One caution, though. While there's no danger to your ears when you do this in a bathtub, it *is* possible to damage your eardrum doing this in a quick depth change in a pool (or a really large bathtub) of as little as four feet. So, just go for depth changes that are enough for you to feel a change in your ears. There's a safe way to change depths in water quickly. You plug your nose, close your mouth, and blow out gently as you submerge. This is called "clearing your ears," and it also works as you go *down* in altitude just in the air.[5]

One more fun thing to do: Take a large coffee can or something similar. Use a hammer and nail to poke three holes in the side of the can, one near the top, one at the middle, and one at the bottom (see Figure 1.2).

Use a strip of duct tape to cover all the holes, and then fill the can with water. Hold the can over a sink or outside, and quickly remove the tape. Notice how strong the water stream is that comes from each of the three holes in the can. There should be a difference between the results at each hole.

Figure 1.2

More science stuff

Figure 1.3

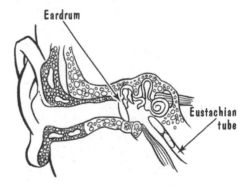

I'm guessing that it's no surprise to you that the reason you felt changes in your ears was due to changes in air pressure and water pressure. To really understand what's going on, it helps to have a basic idea of what the inside of your ear looks like, so take a look at Figure 1.3.

Notice that your **eardrum** separates your inner ear from your outer ear. One side of the eardrum is exposed to the outside of your ear and the outside air. On the other side of the eardrum is something called the **Eustachian tube**, which leads to your sinus cavities, your nose, and your mouth. In other words, this tube connects to the outside air through a different path that goes through your nose and mouth.

Your eardrum is sensitive to differences in pressure on either side of it. When the pressure on the inside of the eardrum is equal to the pressure on the outside of the eardrum, everything feels just fine. If the pressure on one side is greater than the pressure on the other side, the eardrum gets pushed out of its normal position and you get that "stopped up" feeling that can even get a little painful. If the difference in pressure gets too large, your eardrum can rupture, which can't be a good thing.

Before moving on, let's state something that might be relatively obvious:

Areas of high pressure tend to push things
toward areas of low pressure.

---

[5] If this method doesn't work easily for you, don't push it. I'd really hate to get sued because someone broke an eardrum after reading this book!

Works with your eardrum and pretty much everything else.

Given that changes in altitude cause discomfort in your ears, we can assume that changes in altitude result in changes in pressure. Even if you don't want to assume that, just accept it because it's true! Here's what happens: As you go up in altitude (we're talking air, not water here), the outside air pressure gets lower. This makes the pressure inside your eardrum higher than the air pressure outside your eardrum, and your eardrum gets pushed outward. In order for your eardrum to get back to its normal position, the air pressure on the inside of your eardrum has to get lower. That happens once the air pressure inside your Eustachian tube gradually equals the outside air pressure, which you can help along by yawning or chewing gum. Once the air pressure on either side of your eardrum is equalized, you get that "popping" sensation in your ears.

If you're going down in altitude, the reverse happens. As you get to lower altitudes, the outside air pressure increases so it's larger than the air pressure on the inside of your eardrum, causing your eardrum to push inward. Once again, things get back to normal once you use the path through your Eustachian tube to equalize the pressure on the inside and outside of your eardrum. Again, yawning and chewing gum helps. Of course, there's that trick of holding your nose and blowing out gently. This trick (remember, it only works when going down in altitude) is the key to us knowing that increases in altitude decrease air pressure and decreases in altitude increase air pressure. When you hold your nose, close your mouth, and blow out gently, that increases the air pressure in your mouth, nose, and Eustachian tube, because it makes those air molecules inside push harder on your eardrum. Because that equalizes the pressure and makes your ears pop, that means that the air pressure inside the eardrum must have been lower than the outside air pressure before you performed the trick. And that means that as you went down in altitude, the outside air pressure increased. Yes, I realize that last paragraph might have gone by you just a bit too fast, so go ahead and review it slowly. Once you've done that, you should also realize why the "clearing ears" trick doesn't work when going up in altitude. When you go up in altitude, the air pressure inside your eardrum becomes greater than the air pressure outside your eardrum. Blowing gently with your nose plugged increases the air pressure inside your eardrum, and that doesn't help matters, but rather makes them worse.

As we move on to submerging yourself in water, the situation is pretty much the same. The only difference is that the thing causing the pressure on the outside of your eardrum is water rather than air. So we have pressure from the water on the outside of the eardrum and pressure from air (assuming you haven't drowned) on the inside of your eardrum. As before, the trick of "clearing your ears" works only when you submerge in water, not when you come up. That means that water pressure increases the deeper you go.

We have one more bit of evidence that the pressure in water increases as you get deeper. When you poked three holes in a can and filled it with water, you should have found that the stream of water from the bottom hole shot out farther than that from the middle hole, which shot out farther from that from the top hole. The higher the pressure (remember that pressure is force per unit area), the harder it pushes on the water as it leaves the hole. Makes sense, then, that the pressure gets higher and the water pushes harder as you get closer to the bottom of the can, or deeper in the water.

Maybe it's about time we came up with a reason that pressure decreases as you go up, in either water or air, and increases as you go down. The easiest way to think about this is with a swimming pool or other large body of water. What's the main difference between being one foot under a pool of water and being eight feet under a pool of water? Ding, ding, ding... time's up. In the first case you have just a little bit of water above you, and in the second case you have a lot of water above you. You see, the Earth's gravity pulls everything toward it, including water and air, and we call that pull of the Earth's gravity on something its **weight**. When you have a little bit of water above you, you have a little bit of the weight of water pushing on you and your ears. When you have a lot of water above you, you have a lot of the weight of water pushing on you and your ears. A greater push means greater pressure, so that explains what's going on. The pressure you feel when underneath a bunch of water is due to the weight of the water above you. The deeper you go, the more water you have on top of you, and the greater the pressure. In fact, there's a nifty little math relationship that tells you exactly what the pressure will be at a given depth of water. Here it is:

Pressure at a depth h = pressure at the surface + pressure due to the weight of the water above the depth h

Like all such relationships, we can express it with symbols, using P to represent the pressure at depth h, P_0 to represent the pressure at the surface of the water, and a combination of symbols, ρgh, to represent the weight per unit area of the water above the depth h. The symbol ρ is what is known as the **density** of the water, something I'm not going to explain for a couple of chapters, and g is a special number associated with the Earth's gravitational pull. Thus:

$$P = P_0 + \rho gh$$

Now, it's really bad form to just introduce a group of symbols multiplied together, such as ρgh, without making sure you have the experience to understand what they mean, but I'm going to go ahead and ask you to believe that these represent the weight per unit area of the water above a height h. When we get to Chapter 3, I'll explain the whole thing. For now, it will help if you realize that weight per unit area is a pressure, given that weight is the force due to gravity and pressure is force divided by area. Anyway, Figure 1.4 illustrates how the formula works.

All you really need to understand from this formula at this point is that, since $\rho g h$ always is a positive number, the pressure gets greater and greater the deeper you go in a body of water. You should also realize that because we have this nifty formula, we can calculate an exact number for the pressure at any depth of water, an important fact for SCUBA divers and dam builders (see the Applications section).

I told you that water and air, both being considered fluids, are a whole lot alike. Therefore, it shouldn't surprise you that there's a similar formula for determining the air pressure at a given altitude. Just as with water, the air pressure you feel at any height is due to the weight of the air that's above you (see Figure 1.5). For the record, when we talk about the air that's above you, we're referring to all the air that the Earth holds near its surface, otherwise known as the Earth's **atmosphere**.

Figure 1.4

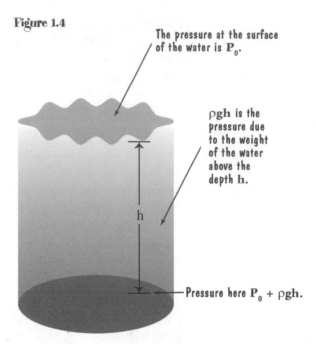

The pressure at the surface of the water is P_0.

$\rho g h$ is the pressure due to the weight of the water above the depth h.

h

Pressure here $P_0 + \rho g h$.

Figure 1.5

The pressure you feel is due to the weight of the atmosphere above you.

SCiLINKS.
THE WORLD'S A CLICK AWAY

Topic: atmosphere

Go to: *www.scilinks.org*

Code: SFAWW02

When dealing with the atmosphere, the pressure gets smaller as you go up in altitude, so the formula is just a bit different. It's

Pressure at a height h = Pressure at the Earth's surface – pressure due to the weight of the air below the height h

In symbol form, we can write this as

$$P = P_0 - \rho g h$$

The only differences between this and our formula for water are that P is the pressure at the *height h*, ρ is the density of *air*, and there's a minus sign because the pressure gets *lower* as you go to greater heights. You *subtract* the pressure due to the weight of the air below you because although that contributes to the air pressure at the surface of the Earth, it doesn't contribute to the air pressure at the height h. Only the air *above* you contributes to that pressure.

Figure 1.6

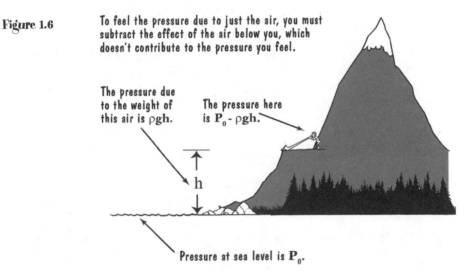

To feel the pressure due to just the air, you must subtract the effect of the air below you, which doesn't contribute to the pressure you feel.

The pressure due to the weight of this air is ρgh.

The pressure here is $P_0 - \rho g h$.

h

Pressure at sea level is P_0.

Even more things to do before you read even more science stuff

We've talked about the pressure at the surface of the Earth due to the weight of the Earth's atmosphere that surrounds the Earth. Time to find out just how large a pressure that is. To do that, you need an empty aluminum pop can, a pan or pie tin of cold water, a pair of tongs large enough to hold the can, and a stove. Keep the pan of cold water (you need just a few centimeters depth of water in the pan—enough to cover the top of the can if you put it in the pan upside down) near the stove.

Put a couple of teaspoons of water in the aluminum pop can, hold it over the flame (or electric heating element) of the stove, and wait until the water inside the

Figure 1.7

upside-down pop can

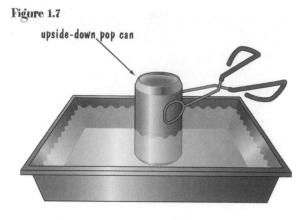

can starts to boil, leading to steam coming out of the top of the can.[6] Once that happens, remove the can from the heat and immediately turn it upside down in the pan of cold water (Figure 1.7) and hold it there. The can should do just a bit of collapsing.

The activity you just did is a lot more dramatic if you use an empty paint thinner can. If you happen to have one of those lying around, great. Put about a half a cup of water in the can and heat it over the stove with the *lid off*. Once the water inside is boiling furiously, remove the can from the stove (use hot pads), quickly put the lid on, and then just set the can in a safe place and watch a great show as the can collapses.

Before I move on to the next section where I explain all of this, I should let you know that there are lots and lots of cool activities to do that relate to air pressure. I'll tell you about them in the next chapter, after we have a really nice scientific model to explain what's going on.

Even more science stuff

When you heat the small amount of water inside a pop can, you heat all of the air inside the can as well. As these air molecules get hotter and hotter, they move faster.[7] As they move faster, a bunch of them escape from the can. The bottom line is that lots of air leaves the can (certainly not all of it), leading to very little air inside the can compared to what's outside the can. Once the air inside the can cools as a result of putting the can in cold water, you end up with regular old atmospheric air pressure (due to the weight of the air above you and the can) on the outside, and not a lot of air pressure on the inside. The dramatic collapse of the soda can (or the paint thinner can if you were able to do that) is an indication that the air pressure around us is pretty darned large. In fact, the atmospheric air pressure at sea level is around 100,000 newtons[8] per square meter (14.7 pounds per square inch).

---

[6] The heating shouldn't take so long that the tongs start to get hot, but if they do, start over using an oven mitt or hot pad to hold the tongs.

---

[7] Lots more detail on what air molecules are doing when you heat them up in the next chapter.

---

[8] A newton is the unit of force in the *Système International* of units. A pound is the unit of force in the English system of units. Scientists generally use the *Système International* of units.

Think about that number for awhile, and you'll realize that we're talking about a *really big* pressure—14.7 pounds of weight hitting every square inch of your body! That might make you wonder about a couple of things. One is how in the world our bodies can withstand that kind of **atmospheric pressure**. The other is how in the world something as light as air can exert such a large pressure. I'll address both of those "how in the world" questions in the Applications section.

By the way, when considering the pressure at a certain depth of water, the value of P_0, which is the pressure at the surface of the water, is often just the atmospheric pressure at the surface of the water.

Chapter Summary

● For many purposes, both air and water can be considered fluids.

● Pressure is force divided by the area over which that force is exerted. We use the concept of pressure extensively in studying air and water because it is an efficient way to deal with the large number of atoms and molecules involved.

● Areas of high pressure push things toward areas of low pressure.

● Atmospheric pressure decreases with altitude and water pressure increases with depth. In both cases, one considers the pressure due to the weight of either air or water above a given position.

● Atmospheric pressure at sea level is about 100,000 newtons per square meter, or 14.7 pounds per square inch.

Applications

1. There are a couple of magic tricks that seem rather amazing, but aren't so amazing once you understand the concept of pressure. One trick is lying on a bed of nails, and the other is walking across a layer of broken glass. In neither case does the magician get hurt. Let's start with the bed of nails. If that bed of nails were instead a single nail, you'd be in trouble. Your entire weight (a force) would be spread out over a very small area. Because pressure is equal to $\frac{force}{area}$

a small area leads to a large pressure. That large pressure would put the single nail right into your body. Now let's turn that single nail into an entire bed of nails. Even though the point of each individual nail has a small area, all of the nails considered together have a rather large surface area. That means the weight of your body is spread out over a large area rather than a small area. With the area being large and being in the denominator of the formula for pressure, the pressure is relatively small. With a small pressure, no nails will be penetrating your gentle skin (Figure 1.8).

A layer of glass is basically the same situation. As long as you have lots and lots of relatively small pieces of glass, the surface area exposed to your foot, and to the weight of your body, is pretty large. Once again, a large surface area leads to a small pressure, and not a lot of blood coming out of your foot.

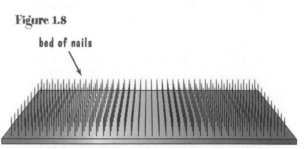

Figure 1.8

bed of nails

Although the point of each nail has a very small surface area, together many nails have a large surface area leading to a relatively small pressure.

2. People who build dams—the ones you build across rivers—know all about water pressure, and that's a good thing. They build dams so they get thicker and thicker as you get toward the bottom of the dam. Why? Because the deeper you go in a body of water, the greater the water pressure. You want the dam thickest where the pressure is the greatest.

3. Maybe you've heard of something called "the **bends**" in association with SCUBA divers.[9] It all has to do with changes in pressure. As you already should know, as you go deeper underwater, the pressure increases. This pressure causes **nitrogen** in your bloodstream and in all other liquids in your body to dissolve. It's the same process one uses to make carbonated beverages, except the gas involved there is carbon dioxide rather than nitrogen. When you shake up a carbonated beverage and open it quickly, you know what happens—the gas escapes all at once and makes a big commotion. If you are SCUBA diving at a great depth and then rise to the surface quickly, the quick change in pressure causes the nitrogen dissolved in your body fluids to escape quickly. That's the bends, and it can be fatal. To counteract this effect, there are guidelines for how quickly a diver can surface safely.

4. One of our "how in the world" questions is the mystery that, with atmospheric pressure at the surface of the Earth being around 100,000 newtons per square meter (about 15 pounds per square inch), our bodies don't collapse under that pressure. The answer is that inside our bodies is an equal pressure pushing outward. Our bodies are about 65% water, and it's the inside pressure of that water plus various gases and even solids such as bones pushing outward that keep us from becoming a mush of over-pressurized gunk.

---

[9] Some say that SCUBA stands for Self Contained Underwater Breathing Apparatus. Others say it stands for Some Come Up Barely Alive.

5. The other "how in the world" question has to do with how something as light as air can produce an atmospheric pressure at the surface of the Earth of 100,000 newtons per square meter. The answer here has to do with just how gosh darned high the atmosphere rises above the surface of the Earth. Although it's impossible to define exactly where the atmosphere ends (there're always *some* air molecules farther away no matter where you decide the cutoff point is), the generally accepted height of the atmosphere is about 600 kilometers, or 372 miles, above the Earth's surface. So, even though a cubic meter of air (one meter on each side of a cube) only weighs around 2–3 pounds (the exact weight depends on temperature and altitude), 600 kilometers of air can weigh quite a bit.[10]

6. For a final application, how about something that people think has a lot to do with air pressure but in fact has almost nothing to do with it? Let's figure out how a **siphon** works so you can steal gasoline from your neighbor's car.[11] Get about a meter's length of tygon tubing (clear plastic tubing—ask at the hardware store) or any other kind of hose-type material. Fill a large pan with water and place it next to a sink so the pan is above the sink. You can also just take the pan of water outside. Next fill your length of tubing with water by submerging it in the pan of water. Make sure there aren't any air bubbles in the tubing. Next seal off one end of the tubing with your finger or thumb and pick the tubing out of the pan of water, as shown in Figure 1.9.

Figure 1.9

None of the water should come out of the tubing. The reason is that the atmospheric pressure at the bottom of the tubing is enough to offset the pressure of the weight of water trying to pull the water out of the tubing. See Figure 1.10.

Now submerge that end you're holding in the pan of water and make sure the open end of the tub-

Figure 1.10

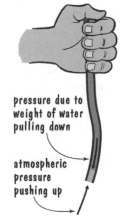

pressure due to weight of water pulling down

atmospheric pressure pushing up

---

[10] This is the weight of a cubic meter of air at the Earth's surface. As you go up in altitude, a cubic meter of air weighs less and less, because the air molecules are farther apart at higher altitudes. Because of this, calculating the weight of the air above you can get a bit complicated, but we're not going to do that calculation, so no need to worry.

---

[11] I probably should state that this is supposed to be a joke, and I am not advocating a life of crime.

Figure 1.11

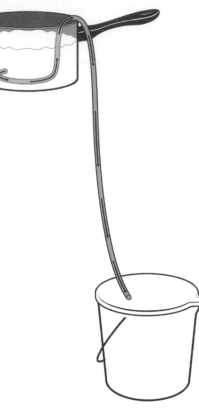

ing is lower than the pan of water. Remove your thumb or finger. As long as you keep the end in the pan submerged and the other end lower than the pan, water will flow through the tubing and out of the pan, as in Figure 1.11.

Now let's analyze this. Once you let go of the end of the tubing that's in the pan of water, you have a pressure exerted on that end. The pressure is due to atmospheric pressure plus any added pressure due to the weight of water that might be above the opening. Because the lower end of the tubing (the one not in the pan) is open to the air, there is also atmospheric pressure at that end. Figure 1.12 illustrates the situation.

Because there isn't a whole lot of height difference between the ends of the tubing, the air pressure at each end is essentially the same. That means there's a *slightly* greater pressure at the end in the pan because of the weight of water above it. That does tend to push water from the pan on out the tubing, but something else is also at work. Because the end of the tubing in the pan is no longer covered, the pressure due to the weight of the water in the tubing is no longer counteracted by atmospheric pressure pushing up (that pressure is now canceled by the atmospheric pressure on the top of the tubing). So, the water simply falls out of the tube. As it falls, it creates low pressure behind it, ensuring that the water in the pan will be pushed into the tube. Note, however, that a si-

Figure 1.12

atmospheric pressure at surface of water

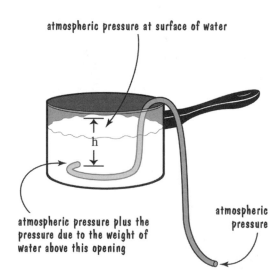

h

atmospheric pressure plus the pressure due to the weight of water above this opening

atmospheric pressure

phon will not work if the open end of the tubing is not lower than the end submerged in the pan. Figure 1.13 should explain why.

Figure 1.13

There's more water in this side of the tubing, resulting in the water flowing out of the pan.

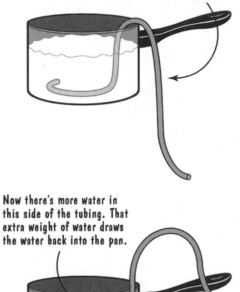

Now there's more water in this side of the tubing. That extra weight of water draws the water back into the pan.

It's a Gas, Gas, Yeah[1]

In this chapter, we're going to delve deeper into air pressure, or to be more correct, the pressure exerted by any gas. The most important part of this chapter is a scientific model for how gases behave, which we'll use to explain earlier things you did with air pressure in addition to a bunch of new exciting activities. Chances are you'll find out that at least a couple of things you've learned previously about gases aren't exactly correct.

---

[1] In case you haven't noticed, I'm keeping with the musical theme in these titles. Not necessarily one of my favorite songs, but it fits.

Things to do before you read the science stuff

Get a plastic water bottle (12 to 16 ounces with a small opening at the top) and put a few centimeters depth of water in the bottle. Place a small, round balloon[2] over the top of the bottle (remove the cap first) so the whole thing looks like Figure 2.1.

As long as you're careful in this next step, there shouldn't be any problems. Hold the bottle over (not touching) a source of heat such as the flame or electric burner on your stove. You should see an almost instant change in the balloon. If not, remove the bottle and check to see that the balloon is tight over the bottle opening. Once you do see the change in the balloon, go ahead and remove the bottle from the heat.[3] After you've removed the bottle and noted the change, place the bottle in the freezer for about a half hour or more.[4] Again note any changes in the balloon when you remove the bottle from the freezer.

Next you need a votive candle, a small pan of water, and a glass that's large enough to fit over the candle but small enough in diameter that it will fit inside the pan. Put about a centimeter's depth of water in the pan and place the candle in the water. Clearly we don't want so much water that it covers the candle (see Figure 2.2).

Figure 2.1

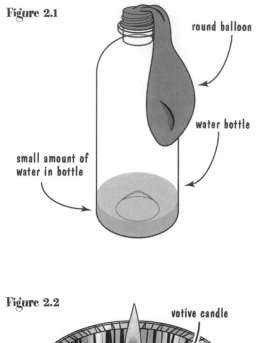

round balloon

water bottle

small amount of water in bottle

Figure 2.2

votive candle

---

[2] There's a good reason for using a round balloon rather than a long and narrow balloon (especially if you demonstrate this for students), which you'll quickly discover if you do this with a long and narrow balloon.

---

[3] As long as you have water in the bottom of the bottle, the bottle shouldn't get anywhere near hot enough to melt the plastic, but don't tempt fate and leave the bottle over the heat source for more than about a minute.

---

[4] If you decide to adapt this for a classroom full of students, you can immerse the bottle in an ice bath instead of putting it in the freezer.

Now light the candle and place the glass upside down in the pan over the candle, as in Figure 2.3. As the candle goes out, you should see something cool happen with the water.

Figure 2.3

This next one is even more dramatic. Get a jar (any size, but larger is better) without a lid. Make yourself a water balloon that's about one and a half times the size of the jar opening. The balloon should sit nicely on top of the jar, as shown in Figure 2.4.

For the next part, be careful and do it near a sink or other readily available source of water or even a fire extinguisher.[5] Remove the balloon from the jar and rip off a small strip of newspaper. Light the edge of the newspaper strip and drop it into the jar. Quickly set the water balloon on top of the jar with the burning paper inside and sit back and watch. Told you it was dramatic!

Figure 2.4

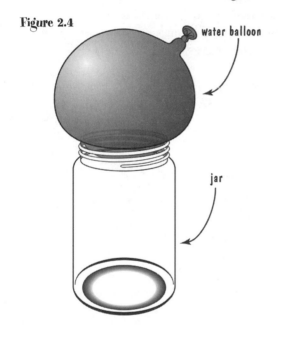

water balloon

jar

The science stuff

To explain what was going on in those activities you just did, we're going to use a scientific model of what gas molecules are doing and how they react to changes in **temperature** and changes in the number of molecules.[6] According to the model, each individual molecule of air or any other gas acts like a billiard ball,

[5] I'm not trying to scare you with this comment, but you are going to start a small fire and it's best to be ready to put a fire out if it gets out of hand. As long as you're careful, there isn't much danger.

[6] This model and how I explain it is almost the same as an explanation provided in Chapter 4 of the *Stop Faking It!* book on Energy, with the exception that I address here what happens if the number of molecules in a confined space changes. Even if you've gone through this explanation in the Energy book, it might not hurt to at least read it through again for review and for the new part of the explanation. Besides, after I present the model, I'll be using it to explain activities that are *not* in the Energy book.

Figure 2.5

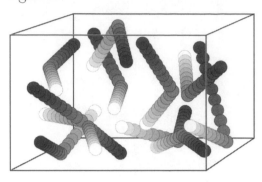

bouncing into other molecules and bouncing off the walls of any container they happen to be in.[7] The hotter these molecules are, the faster they move on average, and the colder they are, the slower they move on average. See Figure 2.5.

To start with, I'll explain the first activity from the previous section using an *incorrect* explanation. The reason for doing this is that the incorrect explanation appears in many places, including textbooks, and I want you to realize why it's wrong.

Incorrect explanation of bottle and balloon: When you first place the balloon over the bottle, the air pressure inside and outside the bottle is equal (this is correct!). The air molecules on the inside of the bottle are, on average, pushing on the balloon just as hard as the air molecules on the outside of the balloon, so it just stays there. When you place the bottle over a heat source, the air molecules inside move faster and require more space in which to move. Because they require more space, they expand and push the balloon outward. When you cool the bottle by placing it in the freezer, the air molecules inside the bottle slow down and don't need as much space as before. Therefore the air inside contracts, causing the balloon to relax or even move inside the bottle.

This is an incorrect explanation because heated gas molecules, although they do move faster when you heat them, do not *need* any more space than they had before. Similarly, although gas molecules do move slower when you cool them down, they do not require less space than before. To demonstrate how gas molecules really behave (the correct explanation), gather about 10 friends and get yourself an open space about the size of a living room. If

SCI*L*INKS.
THE WORLD'S A CLICK AWAY

Topic: atmospheric pressure

Go to: *www.scilinks.org*

Code: SFAWW03

Topic: gas laws

Go to: *www.scilinks.org*

Code: SFAWW04

---

[7] The *correct* model I'm about to explain is known as the **kinetic theory of gases**, and it applies only to what's known as an **ideal gas**. What those words mean is that in this model, we are going to ignore all sorts of internal motions and interactions of the molecules. Given that we are ignoring these kinds of motions and interactions, and given the knowledge that most gases do not behave exactly as an ideal gas, I want to reassure you that the model presented here will work just fine for our purposes. Scientists do this kind of thing all the time. You use the simplest model for your purposes, and that's what we're going to do.

you don't have 10 friends (or students) around, at least read through the activity to get the gist of what's going on.

In the above paragraph, I used the phrase "how gas molecules really behave." As you read those words, keep in mind that what we're talking about is a scientific model—a picture of what's happening on a very small scale. In the big scheme of things, we can't talk about what those molecules are *really* doing, because this is, after all, just a model. Whether or not gas molecules are actually doing what we think they're doing, or whether or not gas molecules themselves even exist, doesn't matter. What matters is whether or not our model explains physical observations and predicts what will happen in any new situation. And that is the true test of any scientific model.

Mark off the boundaries of an area that's maybe 4 meters by 4 meters. Your area can be any shape. Have your group of people stand inside the boundaries. They're going to pretend to be gas molecules, and the boundaries of the area are the walls that confine this gas. At your signal, all of the people-molecules are to begin moving according to the following rules.

● Move in a straight line until you collide with a wall or another gas molecule. In between collisions, always walk in a straight line at a constant speed. Don't alter your path to avoid or to collide with another molecule.

● When you collide (gently!) with a wall or another molecule, bounce off as if you were a billiard ball hitting another ball or the side of a pool table. In other words, try to bounce off so your outgoing angle is equal to your in-coming angle (see Figure 2.6).

● Keep your hands to yourself—no groping! This rule is especially important if you do this activity with adolescents and teens!

Figure 2.6

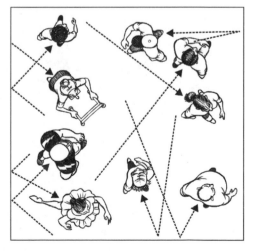

Once the participants understand the rules, go through the following steps and ask the group and yourself the following questions.

1. Have the people start by pretending to be cool gas molecules, moving about slowly. After a bit, ask how much of the available space the molecules use. Another way of stating this is, if the people had wet paint on their shoes, would they eventually paint

the entire area? The answer is yes. The cool gas molecules use all of the available space.

2. Now tell your gas molecules to get hotter, or speed up. Don't let the collisions get too violent! After a bit, stop them and ask how much of the space the molecules used when they were hot. Again, they used all of the space (the whole area would eventually be painted with that paint on their shoes), even though they covered it faster than when they were cool molecules. Did the gas as a whole expand when it got hotter? No, because the gas molecules used the same amount of space, regardless of their speed. Would the gas contract if they became cooler molecules again? No, because they still use all of the available space.

3. Imagine that there's a camera in the ceiling with a really fast shutter speed, so it doesn't show any blurring no matter how fast things are moving. If this camera takes a picture, will you be able to tell from the picture how fast the molecules are moving? Answer: no. The molecules are, on average, the same distance from one another regardless of their speed. Hotter gases (faster moving molecules) do *not* require any more space than cooler gases (slower moving molecules), nor are they on average any farther apart than cooler gas molecules. By the same token, cool gas molecules are, on average, no closer together than hot gas molecules.

Figure 2.7

4. If gases don't necessarily expand when you heat them, and the gas molecules aren't any farther apart on average when you heat them, what's the effect of heating a gas? Because the molecules are moving faster when they're hotter, they hit the walls harder and more often than the molecules of a cool gas. Therefore, a hot gas exerts a greater pressure on the walls than does a cool gas. Important point: If the walls containing the gas are elastic instead of rigid, then heating the gas *will* cause it to expand, because of the increased pressure on the inside of the container pushing out. See Figure 2.7.

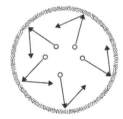

Rigid walls: Faster moving molecules do not cause the walls to expand.

5. Have the people-molecules move around at a medium speed and call attention to the pressure they're exerting on the walls of the container. Then ask half the people to leave the enclosure and ask what happens to the pressure the gas is exerting on the walls. The answer is that the pressure decreases because, although the remaining molecules

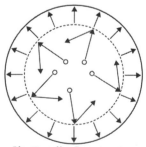

Elastic walls: Faster moving molecules do cause the walls to expand.

are moving just as fast as before, fewer molecules means fewer collisions of molecules with the walls. That means less force per unit area, and less pressure. Have the people who left return, and again ask what happens to the pressure. It increases because with more molecules hitting the walls, the force per unit area, or pressure, increases.

We need one more idea to complete our picture of what gas molecules are doing, which is that areas of higher pressure push things toward areas of lower pressure. That should make sense, especially because I addressed this already in Chapter 1. If something is pushing you with a greater force per unit area than something else, you are going to move toward the something else (Figure 2.8).

Figure 2.8

More force per unit pushes things toward area that exerts less force per unit area.

Correct **explanation of bottle and balloon:** When you first put the balloon on the bottle, the air pressure inside the bottle is equal to the air pressure outside the bottle, so the balloon stays where it is. When you place the bottle over a heat source, two things happen. One is that the air molecules inside the bottle get hotter and move faster. The other is that some of the water molecules evaporate and become **water vapor**—an increase in the number of gas molecules inside the bottle. Both things cause the gas pressure inside the bottle to increase. That makes the pressure inside the bottle greater than the pressure outside the bottle, and the balloon gets pushed outward. When you put the bottle in the freezer, again two things happen. One is that the gas molecules inside the bottle get cooler and move slower. In fact, they move even slower than they did when you first put the balloon on, because then they were at room temperature. The second thing that happens is that those molecules of water vapor inside the bottle once again become water molecules instead of gas molecules. Molecules of water vapor that were already in the bottle before you heated it probably *also* become water molecules, thus decreasing the number of gas molecules inside the bottle. Both things cause the gas pressure inside the bottle to *decrease*, even to the point that the pressure inside the bottle is less than it was before you put the balloon on. Now the pressure inside the bottle is less than it was at the start of the activity, so the balloon gets pushed inside the bottle. Figure 2.9 reviews the entire process.

Now even with that nifty figure to review the process for you, this entire model of how gas molecules behave might still be a bit shaky in your mind. Fortunately, we have a few more activities to explain, helping you solidify your understanding. We'll start with the glass, water, and candle trick. Hopefully, you noticed that as the candle went out, the water in the pan rose up into the glass. Before you light the candle, the air pressure all around your apparatus is pretty much the same, not pushing things one way or the other. That's true even if you put the glass upside down over the unlit candle. Now you light the candle and place the glass over the burning candle. If you wait a bit before putting the glass over the candle, the candle has time to heat the air molecules around it. So, before you put the glass on, the air molecules around the flame are moving faster, but they're also farther apart than the air molecules in the surrounding air. Why? Because those hot air molecules push on the cooler ones around them, creating the extra space. Remember, heating a gas does not necessarily cause the gas to expand. In

Figure 2.9

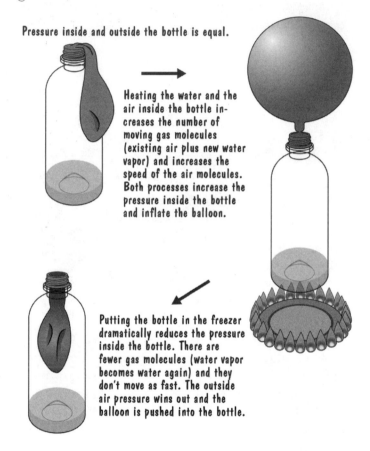

Pressure inside and outside the bottle is equal.

Heating the water and the air inside the bottle increases the number of moving gas molecules (existing air plus new water vapor) and increases the speed of the air molecules. Both processes increase the pressure inside the bottle and inflate the balloon.

Putting the bottle in the freezer dramatically reduces the pressure inside the bottle. There are fewer gas molecules (water vapor becomes water again) and they don't move as fast. The outside air pressure wins out and the balloon is pushed into the bottle.

this case, though, there are no rigid walls to keep the gas from expanding. So, when you first put the glass over the candle, there are fewer air molecules per volume inside the glass (this reduces air pressure) but these molecules are moving faster than the ones outside the glass (this increases air pressure inside). These two effects cancel, and nothing much happens.

While the candle is burning, something else is going on. That something else is that in the process of burning, the candle removes **oxygen** molecules from the air. This is known as **oxidation**. In the process of oxidation, the burning candle removes enough oxygen molecules from the air inside the glass that the pressure inside the glass is significantly reduced[8] (remember that reducing the number of molecules reduces the air pressure). So, because of the initial heating of the air around the candle and be-

Topic: oxidation reduction

Go to: *www.scilinks.org*

Code: SFAWW05

cause of the burning process, you have fewer gas molecules inside the glass than you would have otherwise. Once the candle goes out (not enough oxygen for it to keep burning), your source of heat is gone and the gas molecules inside the glass move slower. At this point, the outside air pressure, which is our normal atmospheric pressure, is much greater than the air pressure inside the glass.

This difference in air pressure pushes the water from the pan up into the glass. Figure 2.10 provides a summary of the process.

On to the water balloon and the jar. Once again, before anything starts burning, the air pressures inside and outside the jar are equal. Then you drop the burning newspaper

Figure 2.10

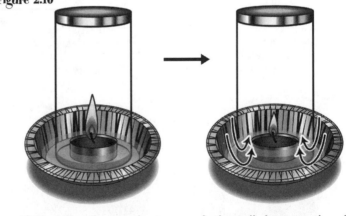

While candle is burning, the air pressure inside and outside the glass is equal. Nothing happens.

As the candle burns out, the reduced number of air molecules inside the glass creates a low-pressure area there. The outside air then pushes the water up into the jar.

---

[8] In case you want the details of this process, it's the paraffin in the candle that's burning. Paraffin combines with oxygen in the air, giving off carbon dioxide (another gas) and water as a result of the chemical reaction. For every 85 oxygen molecules removed from the air, you get 56 carbon dioxide molecules back in the air, and 58 water molecules. Even though some of those water molecules end up as water vapor, there is still a net reduction in the number of gas molecules inside the glass.

into the jar and place the balloon on top. Again, we have competing processes going on inside the jar. The burning paper heats up the air inside, causing the molecules to move faster and increasing the pressure. The burning paper also removes oxygen from the air inside the jar, reducing the pressure inside.[9] Initially, the first process wins out and the pressure inside the jar increases overall. If you watch carefully, you'll notice that the balloon jumps up and down when you first put it on the jar. The jumping is due to the increased air pressure inside the jar, which pushes the balloon up. Of course, as the balloon jumps up, some air molecules escape from the jar, pushed out by the higher air pressure inside the jar. As these molecules leave the jar, they tend to lower the air pressure inside the jar. Each time the balloon jumps, that's because the air pressure inside the jar is larger than the air pressure outside the jar, enough larger that it can lift the balloon. As the balloon lifts, more air molecules escape from inside the jar, decreasing the pressure inside the jar. Eventually, the reduced number of molecules inside the jar (from oxidation and from molecules escaping when the balloon jumps) makes the air pressure inside the jar much smaller than the air pressure outside the jar. Also, the flame goes out, removing the source of heat inside the jar. At that point, the outside air pressure pushes the balloon into the jar. See Figure 2.11 for a summary.

Figure 2.11

The burning paper increases the pressure inside the jar. This pushes the balloon up, allowing the air to escape.

Reduced air pressure inside the jar, as a result of a reduced number of air molecules, allows the balloon to fall back into place.

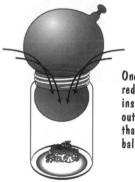

Once the fire is out, the greatly reduced number of air molecules inside the jar means that the outside pressure is much greater than the inside pressure. The balloon is pushed into the jar.

---

[9] This is almost identical to the burning of paraffin in the previous activity. Molecules in the paper combine with oxygen to produce carbon dioxide and water, with a net reduction in the number of gas molecules. You should notice the water forming on the sides of the jar.

Here I should give a nod to an ex-colleague named Bryce Hixon, who founded the now-defunct Wild Goose Company. As far as I know, he coined the phrase "science never sucks." What that phrase means is that vacuums and other devices, such as jars with burning paper in them, never *suck* an object from one place to another. It's always differences in pressure that *push* an object or substance from one place to another. So no, you don't "suck" a liquid through a straw, as explained in the Applications section of this chapter.

Let's see ... one more activity to explain, this one from the first chapter. To demonstrate the large magnitude of atmospheric pressure, I had you heat up a small amount of water in an aluminum can and then place that can upside down in a pan of cool water. The can collapsed. You can probably explain this on your own by now, but just in case you're not quite ready, here's an explanation. When you heat the can, you cause water molecules to become water vapor (this increases the pressure inside the can) and you heat up the air molecules inside the can (this also increases the pressure inside the can). Because the can is open, this increased pressure inside the can pushes air molecules out of the can. As you let the heating continue, lots of gas molecules escape the can, enough so that, when you remove the can from the source of heat, the air pressure inside the can is significantly lower than the normal outside atmospheric pressure. When you place the can upside down in the water, you seal off the can and the differences in air pressure do their thing.

More things to do before you read more science stuff

Take a regular old 8½- by 11-inch piece of paper and hold it as shown in Figure 2.12. Blow across the top and see what happens. Does the paper do what you expect?

Figure 2.12

8½" x 11" sheet of paper

Next fold the same piece of paper in half, making a tent, and place it on a table with a smooth surface. Predict what will happen when you blow through the tent, and then do it, as shown in Figure 2.13.

Figure 2.13

Finally, get two empty aluminum cans and place them on a bed of straws, as in Figure 2.14. Blow between the cans and see what happens. All of these activities are related, so why not move on to the next section and figure out what's going on?

Figure 2.14

More science stuff

Before getting to an explanation, let's agree on what happened in those activities. The sheet of paper should have moved upward when you blew across the top, the paper tent should have collapsed when you blew through the center, and the two aluminum cans should have come together when you blew between them. If those things didn't happen, refer back to the drawings and try again.

To figure out what's going on, let's examine the paper tent. After you set up the tent and before you do any blowing, the air pressure inside and outside the tent is equal, and the paper doesn't go anywhere. Also, and this is part of our model I haven't yet told you about, the molecules of air inside and outside the tent are in random motion. They are just as likely to be moving in one direction as another. See Figure 2.15.

Now you blow through the center of the paper tent. Your breath creates a different situation inside the tent. Instead of the air molecules moving about randomly inside the tent, a whole bunch of them are now moving parallel to the tent, as in Figure 2.16.

Figure 2.15

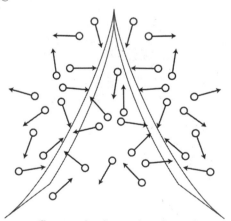

The air molecules inside and outside the paper tent are in random motion.

Figure 2.16

Air molecules inside the tent tend to move parallel to the sides of the tent because you're blowing them that way.

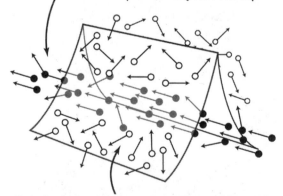

Air molecules outside the tent are still in random motion.

In this situation, many fewer air molecules inside the tent are directed at the tent than before. This means that the air pressure against the inside of the paper tent is lower than the air pressure against the outside of the paper tent. Therefore, the paper tent collapses.

This effect is known as the **Bernoulli Effect**, named after Daniel Bernoulli, a physicist who explained this phenomenon in 1738. In short, faster moving air (or water, too) generates an area of low pressure. Before I move on and explain the other activities, I'd like to mention how the Bernoulli Effect is treated in most physics textbooks. Those books introduce lots of principles and associated formulas, among them something called *conservation of energy*, which one can apply to various physical situations. When applying these principles to moving air or moving water, one can see *in the math* that the pressure is lower where the fluid is moving faster, and that's the end of the story. These books seldom bother to explain what's going on in terms of what the molecules are doing, which is one of the reasons I'm writing this book series. Demand of yourself, and of anyone or anything trying to teach you science concepts, that those concepts make sense. That's the only way to get through teaching science while keeping your sanity![10]

On to the next two activities. When you blow across the top of a piece of 8½- by 11-inch paper, it moves upward. The reason is that again, you are causing many of the molecules on top of the paper to move parallel to the paper rather

Figure 2.17

Pressure pushing outward on the tent is much smaller than the pressure pushing inward on the tent.

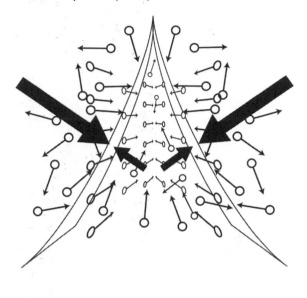

Topic: Bernoulli's Principle

Go to: *www.scilinks.org*

Code: SFAWW06

---

[10] For the record, it took a long time for me to come to this conclusion. Until I started teaching science concepts on my own, I had no idea I had been memorizing most concepts rather than understanding them. Memorizing makes you feel uncomfortable when explaining ideas. Understanding provides lots of comfort. After you've had the chance to experience both options, which option to choose is a no-brainer.

than toward it. This reduces the air pressure on the top of the paper, causing the higher pressure underneath to push the paper upwards. Check out Figure 2.18.

I'm going to make the bold assumption that you can figure out on your own what happened with the two aluminum cans sitting on the straws. Fast moving air in between, lower pressure as a result, and the cans move together. Easy by now, huh?

Figure 2.18

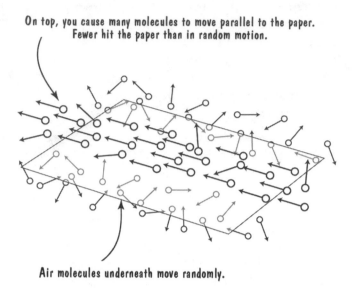

On top, you cause many molecules to move parallel to the paper. Fewer hit the paper than in random motion.

Air molecules underneath move randomly.

Chapter Summary

- The kinetic theory of gases is a scientific model that helps explain the behavior of gases. In this model, gas molecules behave a lot like colliding billiard balls.

- Changing the temperature of gas molecules (and thus their speed) and/or the number of gas molecules in a given volume changes the pressure exerted by the gas.

- Hot gas molecules do not require any more space than cool gas molecules, and cool gas molecules do not require any less space than hot gas molecules.

- Whether gases expand or contract, or don't change volume at all, when heated or cooled depends largely on what surrounds the gas.

- Increasing the speed of fluids (both water and air) in a specific direction decreases the pressure the fluids exert in a direction perpendicular to the direction of the increased speed. This is known as the Bernoulli Effect.

Applications

1. Place a fold-lock or ziplock plastic bag over a glass and push the bag in the glass a bit, as shown in Figure 2.19. Then place a rubber band around the bag

so it's secure. Once the rubber band is nice and tight, pull the center of the plastic bag upwards, as shown in the right side of Figure 2.19. Doesn't work very well, does it?

Figure 2.19

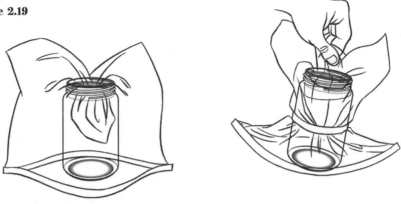

As with most of our previous activities with air pressure, the air pressure inside and outside the bag are equal to start with. When you pull up on the bag, it moves easily at first. Then it becomes nearly impossible to pull it farther. What you have done by pulling up the plastic bag initially is create more room for the air molecules inside the glass. Because of the rubber band, however, no air molecules go in or out of the glass. By creating more room for those molecules inside, you are reducing the number of collisions they make with the glass and the plastic bag. That reduces the pressure inside. There's no change in temperature or number of molecules inside, so there's nothing to increase the pressure inside. Therefore, when you pull the plastic bag up, you get to a point where the outside air pressure is greater than the inside air pressure, so you can't go any farther.

2. I mentioned earlier that you don't "suck" liquid through a straw. Instead, you create a low-pressure area inside your mouth. That allows the outside air pressure to *push* the liquid from the glass, up through the straw, into your mouth. As a by-product, outside air pressure pushes your cheeks in toward the lower pressure inside your mouth. And now for the question I know is right on the tip of your tongue—can I drink through a straw on the Moon? Nope. Two reasons for that. The first is that if you lift your space helmet to drink through a straw, you'll die from lack of oxygen and the pressure inside the space suit will push your head out in a not-so-gracious fashion. The second is that there is very little atmospheric pressure on the Moon (very few air molecules). So, no matter how much you lower the air pressure inside your mouth, there isn't enough atmospheric pressure to push the liquid up the straw.

3. Next magic trick. Fill a glass up to the rim with water. Place an index card over the top, as shown in Figure 2.20.

   Over a sink (just in case the trick doesn't work), quickly turn the whole contraption upside down, holding on to the index card as you do. Then release the card. If everything does what it's supposed to, the card will stay where it is. Impressive. The explanation for this includes a concept known as *surface tension*, but given that I'm not going to address that concept until later in the book, we'll just focus on what's happening with the air pressure, or lack thereof. Ordinarily, you would expect the weight of the water to push down on the index card hard enough that the card falls off and the water follows. If you watch the whole thing carefully, though, you'll notice that a small "air" space forms in the top (formerly the bottom) of the glass when you turn the glass over. See Figure 2.21.

   Actually, there is very little air in that space in the glass. Unless you turn the glass over very slowly, and don't hold tightly onto

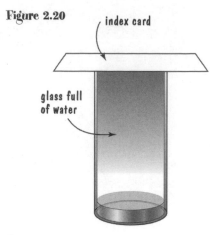

Figure 2.20

index card

glass full of water

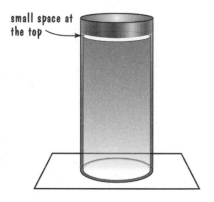

Figure 2.21

small space at the top

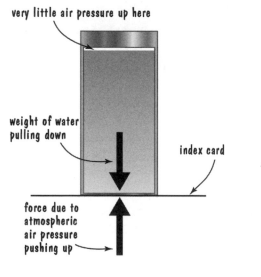

Figure 2.22

very little air pressure up here

weight of water pulling down

index card

force due to atmospheric air pressure pushing up

the card, there isn't a chance for much air to get into that space. With very few air molecules in that space, you have very little air pressure. There is so little air pressure in that space, in fact, that the difference between the outside air pressure and the small air pressure in that space is enough to hold up the weight of the water in the glass. Therefore, the water stays where it is. See Figure 2.22.

4. If you've ever used a portable gas can, you know that there are two openings in the can. One is the main spout and the other is a small hole on the opposite end with a small cap over it. If you try to pour gas out without removing the cap from the

small hole, things will work fine for a while and then not so well. With the small hole closed, the more gas you pour out of the spout the more you are creating a situation where the outside air pressure is greater than the air pressure inside the can. That keeps gas from coming out of the can. Simply loosening the cap on the small hole will introduce atmospheric pressure to the inside of the can, and the pouring is much easier.

5. One situation most often associated with the Bernoulli Effect is the lift on airplane wings, so here's that explanation. For starters, you ought to know that most of the lift airplanes get has nothing to do with the Bernoulli Effect. Most of the lift airplanes get is due to air molecules hitting the wings directly from below, pushing the plane upward. That said, here's how Bernoulli enters the picture. Airplane wings are shaped as shown in Figure 2.23.

Figure 2.23

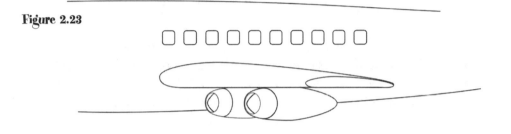

As the airplane moves through the air, air molecules move over both the top and bottom of the wing. If we assume there are no irregularities in the flow of the air (actually not a great assumption, but good enough for our purposes), the air flowing over the top of the wing ends up at the back of the wing in the same time as the air flowing under the bottom of the wing. Because the air flowing over the top has to travel a greater distance, it must move faster than the air moving under the wing (Figure 2.24).

Figure 2.24   The air moving over the top has to travel a greater distance in the same amount of time. Therefore, it moves faster.

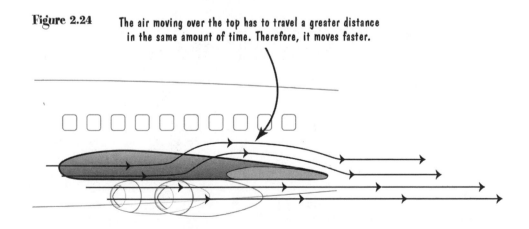

Because the air moving over the top of the wing moves faster than the air moving underneath the wing, the air pressure above the wing is lower than the air pressure below the wing. That's the Bernoulli Effect. The result is an upward lift, as shown in Figure 2.25.

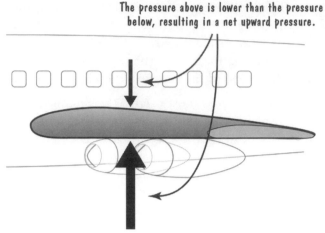

Figure 2.25

The pressure above is lower than the pressure below, resulting in a net upward pressure.

Now the thing that always bothered me about this explanation was why in the world the air traveling over the top of the wing had to traverse that route in the same time it took the air to move underneath the wing. I read things like "laminar flow" and such, but never really understood what was going on. I've thought about the situation, and here's my take on it.[11] Let's think first about the plane not moving. The air pressure all around the wing is equal. Now the plane starts moving. What might happen if the air above the wing and below the wing moved at the same speed? If that happened, there would be, at least instantaneously, a "gap" of air molecules toward the back of the top of the wing (Figure 2.26).

Figure 2.26

If the air above and below moved at the same speed there would be a "gap" where the air above lags behind.

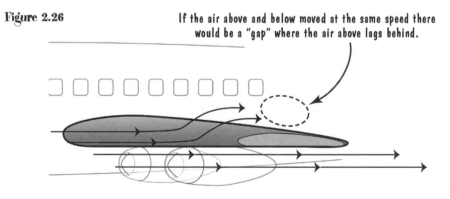

---

[11] It might seem odd for an author of a science book to say something like, "I've thought about it, and here's my take." Believe it or not, there are a whole bunch of phenomena that are not explained in science books. Sometimes you just have to use what knowledge you have to figure out a situation. I have never run across a good explanation of this particular situation, hence my statement that this is "my take." I could be wrong on this one, and if I am, then I'm sure someone will come forward with a better explanation and we'll correct it in the second printing!

As we already know, fewer air molecules (what you have in that gap) result in a lower air pressure. This situation means that air molecules will be pushed into that gap by the outside air pressure. That push increases the speed of the air molecules above the wing, and gives us our resulting Bernoulli Effect. See Figure 2.27.

Figure 2.27

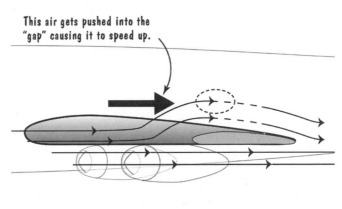

This air gets pushed into the "gap" causing it to speed up.

6. The applications of the Bernoulli Effect are many. Here are a few. Take a Ping-Pong ball and put it in a funnel. Hold it as shown in Figure 2.28 and try to blow the Ping-Pong ball out of the funnel. Won't happen.

Next hold the funnel and Ping-Pong ball upside down, holding the Ping-Pong ball in the funnel, as in Figure 2.29. Begin blowing and then remove your hand so you're no longer holding the Ping-Pong ball in the funnel.

Figure 2.28

Figure 2.29

Figure 2.30

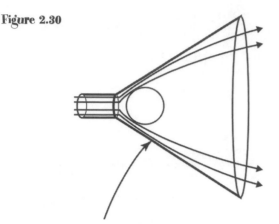

Fast-moving air moving around the ball creates a low-pressure area that keeps the ball in the funnel.

As long as you keep blowing, the ball should remain where it is. Figure 2.30 shows what's going on. When you blow through the funnel, the fast-moving air that goes around the Ping-Pong ball creates a low-pressure area. The resulting difference in high and low air pressure keeps the ball in the funnel, whether you're trying to blow the ball out upward or downward.

Prairie dogs know all about the Bernoulli Effect. They build their homes with a mound by one entrance and no mound by the second entrance. As air flows over the mound by the one entrance, it speeds up (see the shape of the airplane wing in Application 3). That creates an area of low pressure. The difference in air pressure between the entrance with no mound and the entrance with a mound pushes air through the prairie dogs' burrow (Figure 2.31). Instant air conditioning!

Finally, the Bernoulli Effect comes into play when you're driving in your car. If you're rolling down the freeway and open a window, be prepared for loose papers and such to head for the open window. The reason is that, with the window open, you have fast moving air just outside the window (low-pressure area because of the Bernoulli Effect) and still air (higher air pressure because the air isn't moving) inside the car. Things inside the car get pushed to the outside of the car. Smokers know this because when

Figure 2.31

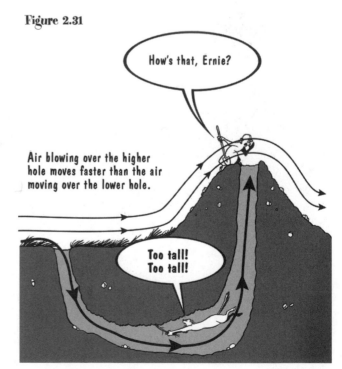

How's that, Ernie?

Air blowing over the higher hole moves faster than the air moving over the lower hole.

Too tall! Too tall!

they crack just one window, the smoke gets pushed toward that low-pressure opening and out of the car (Figure 2.32). Because the windows themselves get pushed out due to the difference in air pressure, sometimes a window that's been rolled down won't go all the way up (while you're moving) because it just doesn't line up properly.

Figure 2.32

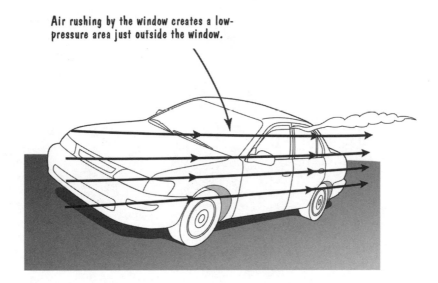

Air rushing by the window creates a low-pressure area just outside the window.

7. This application of the Bernoulli Effect deserves its own number. When you flush a toilet, why does everything go down into the pipes and eventually the sewer? Part has to do with gravity, but part has to do with Bernoulli. Take a close look at your toilet, and you'll see that there's a small hole in the bowl that's forward of the main exit. Flush the toilet and you'll notice that water rushes out of that small hole during the flush. Fast rushing water out of that opening creates a low-pressure area (Bernoulli Effect!), helping to draw whatever is in the toilet further down into the sewer. Science is wonderful.

Balloons and Other Things That Sometimes Float

Hot air balloons float—sometimes. Regular old balloons that you get at a party float—sometimes. Boats float—sometimes. What makes them float and what makes them sink? How can a boat made of steel float but a solid chunk of steel sink to the bottom of the ocean? Part of the answer has to do with something called density, which I promised earlier I would explain to you. That and more in this chapter. And yes, the concepts we're going to deal with in this chapter *do* have a lot to do with weather.

"Archimedes, I say it will. . .float. No! Wait...Sink...No, float...Sink?..."

Things to do before you read the science stuff

Head to your local hobby or craft store and get a package of really small re-sealable plastic bags, ones that are about 3 cm by 5 cm. Also get a package of slotted craft sticks, which are basically popsicle sticks with slots in them. Yes, they'll have them! After that get a couple of paper clips, some rubbing alcohol,[1] some vegetable oil, and a supply of water.

Figure 3.1

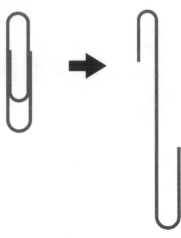

Bend each of your paper clips into the shape shown in Figure 3.1.

Poke one end of two of the paper clips through the top portion, above the re-sealable part, of two of the plastic bags. The idea here is that you can have a plastic bag hanging from a paper clip while not disturbing the contents sealed inside the plastic bag. Using two extra craft sticks held together, create a "balance" that will hold a plastic bag on each end. With one empty plastic bag on each end of the slotted craft stick and with you holding the craft stick in the center using two extra craft sticks, everything should be in balance. Take a look at Figure 3.2.[2]

Figure 3.2

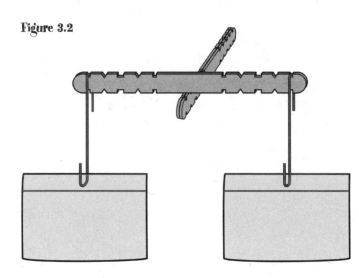

Before continuing, see whether or not you agree with the following statements: (1) Providing you support the stick exactly in the middle, providing the two plastic bags and their contents weigh the same, and providing you hang the

---

[1] Rubbing alcohol is highly flammable, so make sure you don't have any open flames around. If you plan on doing this activity with students, first check the safety guidelines of your school, because the use of rubbing alcohol might be banned.

---

[2] Credit goes to Greg Martinez of Quincy High School in Quincy, WA, for figuring out how to get this contraption to balance easily. I was using a third, bent paper clip to support the craft stick, and it wasn't working very well!

bags the same distance from the center balance point, then the stick will be in balance and not tip one way or the other. (2) If one bag is heavier than the other, then the stick will tip downward on that bag's side of the stick.

If you agree with those statements, then we're set to move on. If you don't agree with those statements, then you'll have to spend the night in the box and get your mind right,[3] because those statements are the truth.

Start by filling two bags with water and putting them on your craft stick balance. Do they weigh the same? In other words, does the contraption stay in balance with water-filled bags on each end of the stick? It should, more or less. A tiny tilt one way or another shouldn't be a big deal.

Next fill one bag with water and the other with vegetable oil. Place them on either end of your balance and see what happens. Then compare a bag filled with water with a bag filled with rubbing alcohol, and finally compare a bag filled with vegetable oil with a bag filled with rubbing alcohol. Keep track of which bags of liquid are heavier than other bags of liquid.

The science stuff

If you didn't actually compare the weights of those bags filled with liquids, then shame on you. Yes, I'll tell you what should have happened, but there's no substitute for doing the activities so you have the experience from which to understand concepts. That said, here's what you should have observed: The bag of alcohol weighed less than the bag of water. The bag of vegetable oil also weighed less than the bag of water. The difference between the oil and alcohol might have been more difficult to detect, but if you do it a few times, you should notice a tendency for the bag of vegetable oil to weigh more than the bag of alcohol.

So what does this mean? What it means is that a given volume of liquid has a different weight depending on the liquid. **Volume** refers to the amount of space taken up by something. Because each bag is the same size, when you fill up the bags to the top, you are creating the same volume of each liquid. There's a number you can assign to how much a given volume of any substance weighs, and it's called **density**. The greater the density of a substance, the more a given volume of that substance weighs.

Now before going on, I have to make a distinction between two concepts—**mass** and **weight**. The weight of an object is the *force* that the Earth exerts on the object due to the Earth's gravitational pull. The mass of an object is some-

---

[3] Relatively obscure reference to the movie *Cool Hand Luke*.

SCi
LINKS.
THE WORLD'S A CLICK AWAY

Topic: density

Go to: *www.scilinks.org*

Code: SFAWW07

Topic: mass and volume

Go to: *www.scilinks.org*

Code: SFAWW08

Topic: mass/weight

Go to: *www.scilinks.org*

Code: SFAWW09

thing different. In order to get a solid grasp of the difference between the two concepts, you have to understand Newton's first law.[4] I'm not going to explain that here, so I'll give you a quick and dirty distinction between the two quantities. Mass can be thought of as the "amount of stuff" contained in any object or substance, while weight is the force of gravity acting on the object or substance. You can take an object anywhere in the universe and its mass will not change. Because gravitational forces get weaker with distance, though, the weight of something *will* change the farther you get away from the Earth.

Okay, so why am I making that distinction? Because although there is something known as **weight density**, for the rest of this book we're going to use the concept of **mass density**, which is how much mass a given volume of substance has. Here's the definition.

$$\text{mass density} = \frac{\text{mass of an object or substance}}{\text{volume of the object or substance}}$$

That relationship expressed in symbols is

$$\rho = \frac{m}{V}$$

where ρ is the Greek letter "rho" (pronounced as in "row, row, row your boat"), m represents mass, and V represents volume. The reason V is capitalized here is so you don't confuse it with a lower case v, which generally refers to velocity. Now, because each of the little baggies held the same volume of fluid, the relative weights of those baggies of fluid are the same as the relative densities of the fluids. We can conclude that the density of alcohol is less than the density of vegetable oil, which is less than the density of water.

I don't want you to get too hung up on the difference between mass density and weight density. As long as you're dealing with things near the surface of the Earth, those two quantities give you basically the same kind of information. For example, when comparing the weights of a bag of water and a bag of vegetable oil, you found that the water has a greater weight density than the

---

[4] See the *Stop Faking It!* book on Force and Motion for a detailed explanation.

vegetable oil. The mass densities of the two substances also have the same relationship, so we can simply say that water is denser than vegetable oil. Also, water is denser than rubbing alcohol, and vegetable oil is denser than rubbing alcohol. If you think of the density of a substance as telling you something about how "closely packed" the atoms or molecules of the substance are, you are on the right track.

Let's see if this definition of density makes sense in terms of what we discussed in Chapter 1. There, we learned that the pressure at a depth h in a liquid is given by $P = P_0 + \rho gh$, where P_0 is the pressure at the surface of the liquid and ρ is the density of the liquid. The larger ρ is, the denser the liquid and the more a column of that liquid will weigh. Makes sense that this will create a greater pressure at the depth h. So, if you SCUBA dive in either vegetable oil or rubbing alcohol (neither is recommended!), the pressure won't increase as quickly when you submerge as it will in water. For that matter, saltwater is denser than fresh water (the dissolved salt makes for a more closely packed substance), so changes in pressure with depth are different in the two kinds of water. That affects calculations you might make when determining how fast you can surface without getting the "bends."

More things to do before you read more science stuff

Here's hoping you still have the water, oil, and alcohol around. Get a clear drinking glass and pour a small amount of water into it. Then slowly pour a layer of vegetable oil on top of the water. To make sure the liquids don't mix, you can pour the oil down the side of a tilted glass or pour it over the back of a spoon held just above the water's surface. The liquids should remain separate. Which liquid floats on which? Repeat this little demonstration using vegetable oil and alcohol (rinse the glass thoroughly first) and water and alcohol (again rinse first). Because the water and alcohol are both clear, it's a little bit difficult to see the separation of the liquids, but it's there.

Now get a cork, a Styrofoam ball, a ball of modeling clay, and a small rock. Drop each of these into a glass of water and see what happens. Of course, you probably know what will happen before you start. The cork and Styrofoam ball will float and the rock and ball of modeling clay will sink. Can you figure out why?

Next get two different colors of food coloring, some very hot water, and some very cold water. Put one color of food coloring in the hot water and the other color in the cold water. Pour the hot and cold water into a new, empty, clean glass and observe. Again it helps to pour one liquid in the new glass and then pour the other one down the side of the glass.

More science stuff

First you have to recall that we discovered that alcohol is less dense than vegetable oil, which is less dense than water. You saw that when comparing the weights of tiny plastic bags containing equal volumes of the liquids. Once you recall that, you should agree with the following statement.

Less dense substances tend to float on top of denser substances.

Makes sense. The less dense alcohol floats on top of the denser vegetable oil, and the less dense vegetable oil tends to float on the denser water. Also, the cork and the Styrofoam are less dense than water, so they float on the water. A ball of modeling clay and a rock are denser than water, so they sink. I need to warn you right now that a difference in densities is only part of the reason why one liquid or object floats on another liquid. You don't have to look any further than steel ships to see that there's more to it than density. Steel is much denser than water, yet these ships float just fine. Not to worry, because I'll explain the whole picture by the time this chapter is done.

Let's see if we can figure out one reason why less dense substances tend to float on top of denser substances. Well, the reason is gravity. The Earth pulls on all things, and we call that force gravity. The force of gravity on something[5] depends on how much *mass* is in the something, so things that are denser (more mass per unit volume) tend to have a greater gravitational force exerted on them than things that are less dense. Now, these substances (let's think liquids) also exert forces on each other, but all other things being equal, gravity wins out. That means that dense liquids sink to the bottom and less dense liquids are left on top. That also explains, at least in part, why balls of modeling clay and rocks sink in water.

To end this section, let's talk about why exactly various liquids have different densities and float on other liquids, and why hot water is less dense than cold water and thus tends to float on top of cold water. Various liquids are composed of different molecules. The molecules in water are relatively small (just an oxygen and two hydrogens), so it's easy for them to be packed closely together. Molecules of vegetable oil, however, are rather large and have rather complicated shapes. These restrictions make it more difficult to pack vegetable oil molecules closely together. Thus, they tend to take up more space, making the density of vegetable oil less than that of water.

---

[5] You might remember that the force that gravity exerts on something is called the something's *weight*.

To move on, obviously the hot water is less dense than the cold water. We know that because hot water floats on top of cold water. The reason has to do with what the water molecules do as you heat them up or cool them down. We learned in Chapter 2 that *gas* molecules can take up more or less space depending on their temperature and the nature of their surroundings. Liquid molecules are similar, because as you heat them, they move around more and the liquid expands into the available space.[6] When they create more space for themselves, the overall density of the liquid decreases (same mass in more space). Hot water molecules move around more than cold molecules, so hot water molecules are less dense than cold water molecules. Hence, when you mix hot and cold water, the cold water will always end up on the bottom.

Finally, recall that in this book we consider air to be a fluid. What do you suppose happens when you mix hot and cold air in the atmosphere? Well, there are no walls to speak of containing the air (actually, other air molecules can be considered sort of a wall, but they are able to move), so heated air tends to create more room for itself. That means that hot air is less dense than cold air. So, the natural tendency is for hot air to "float" on top of cold air. Seems like a simple point, but as you'll see later, it has big time implications for weather patterns, the direction of winds, and many other things.

Even more things to do before you read more science stuff

Still have a slotted craft stick with the paper clips around? If not, make another apparatus just as in Figure 3.2, but replace the small plastic bags with metal washers that are of equal size. You should have something like Figure 3.3, with the whole thing in balance because the washers have equal weight.

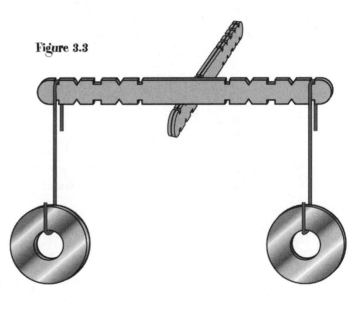

Figure 3.3

---

[6] Important point here. I talked in Chapter 2 about gas molecules *not* taking up more space when they're heated, as long as the gas molecules are confined in a closed space. Here we are talking about heating liquids that have all the room they need in order to expand.

Figure 3.4

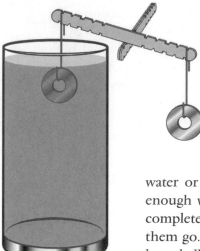

Get a glass of water and dip one of the washers in the water so the washer is submerged, but the craft stick isn't touching the side of the glass. Things don't stay in balance, do they? (See Figure 3.4.)

Now get two balloons of equal size, so they weigh pretty much the same. Blow up one of the balloons just a little bit and blow the other one up a lot, tying both of them off. If we ignore the differing amounts of air in each balloon, they still have about the same weight, right? Fill a sink with water or wait until the next time you take a bath. You need enough water so that both the large and small balloon can be completely submerged. Submerge both of them and then let them go. Which one jumps up higher, the small balloon or the large balloon?

Figure 3.5

Finally, get a Styrofoam ball that will fit inside a clear glass. Straighten a large paper clip so you can shove it all the way through the center of the Styrofoam ball. The relative sizes of the paper clip and Styrofoam ball should be such that the paper clip sticks out of each end of the ball. Use pliers to put a slight bend in the part of the paper clip protruding through one side (this will hold the paper clip in place) and create a small hook on the other end of the protruding paper clip. Check out Figure 3.5.

Figure 3.6

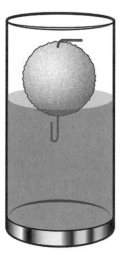

Get several metal washers that are all the same size. Fill a clear glass half full of water and place the Styrofoam ball without any washers attached into the water. (See Figure 3.6.) Using masking tape or a washable marker, mark the water level on the outside of the glass.

Remove the ball. Add a washer to the bottom hook in the paper clip and place the ball, paper clip, and washer back in the water, and note what happens to the water level in the glass. Remove the Styrofoam ball from the water, add a second washer to the bottom hook, and replace the ball in the water. Again mark the water level. Continue doing this (adding washers and replacing) until the Styrofoam ball sinks or the water flows over the edge of the glass.

Finally, get two identical, clear drinking glasses. Fill one about half full with water. Fill the other one with vegetable oil until it has exactly the same amount of oil as the other glass has water (see Figure 3.7). Put them side-by-side. Mark the level of fluid in each glass with a washable marker or with masking tape.

Take your Styrofoam ball with the paper clip through it and with a couple of washers hanging on the end. Place this in the glass of water, and mark the change in water level. Then place the ball in the vegetable oil and mark the change in the level of the oil. Compare the two changes.

Figure 3.7

water

100% pure vegetable oil (honest!)

Even more science stuff

Lots to explain here. We'll start with the two washers balanced on the craft stick, followed by you submerging one of the washers in a glass of water. Your craft stick undoubtedly tipped down on the side of the washer not in the water. One way of explaining this is to say that "objects weigh less in water." Not a bad idea. If you believed this, then you would have to undertake a bunch of experiments to show that the force of gravity (an object's weight) somehow gets smaller when an object is submersed in water. I honestly don't know if anyone has done such experiments, but since we can't justify that view of things, we have to reach another conclusion. That conclusion is that any object immersed in a fluid experiences an upward force. That upward force, called the **buoyant force**, opposes the gravitational force, and gives us a situation something like Figure 3.8.

Figure 3.8

buoyant force

gravitational force

 SCI LINKS.
THE WORLD'S A CLICK AWAY

Topic: buoyant force

Go to: *www.scilinks.org*

Code: SFAWW10

Figure 3.8 shows the buoyant force as being equal to the gravitational force. If this is the case, the object will float in the fluid. If the gravitational force is greater than the buoyant force, the object will sink. If the buoyant force is greater than the gravitational force, the object will accelerate (speed up) upwards. This was the situation when you submerged

Figure 3.9

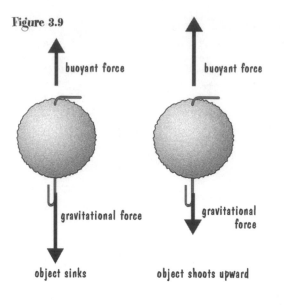

the balloons completely in water and let go. Figure 3.9 shows what happens when the gravitational force and buoyant force are not equal.

At the end of this section, I'll discuss why it makes sense that a fluid exerts an upward force on objects submerged in it. Before that, though, let's explain the other things you observed. You submerged equal-weight balloons in water, and I hope you saw that the large balloon jumped above the water surface higher than the small balloon, as in Figure 3.10.

Figure 3.10

The large balloon shoots up higher than the small balloon.

Because their weights are equal, the only explanation for this is that the buoyant force acting on the large balloon must be larger than the buoyant force acting on the small balloon (Figure 3.11).

What that means is the following:

The buoyant force acting on an object depends on how much fluid it displaces. If the object displaces more fluid, then it will experience a larger buoyant force.

Figure 3.11

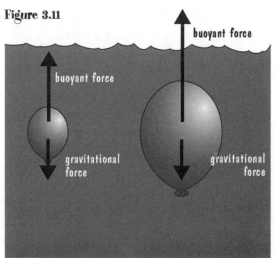

That's supported by the next activity you did, adding washers to the Styrofoam ball floating in a glass of water. As you added washers, you displaced more water as evidenced by the water level in the glass rising with added washers. If you do this activity carefully and measure carefully the rise in height of the water in the glass, you'll find that doubling the weight doubles the amount of water displaced and tripling the weight triples the amount of water displaced.[7] Figure 3.12 explains what's going on.

Figure 3.12

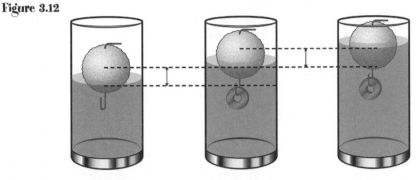

Doubling the weight (approximately) doubles the water displacement.

So, we know that objects immersed in fluids experience an upward buoyant force. We also know that the size of the force depends on how much fluid the object displaces—the more fluid displaced, the larger the buoyant force. There's one more piece to the explanation, though. It has to do with the last activity you did in the previous section. When you placed your Styrofoam ball with washers into the glass of water and then in the glass of vegetable oil, you should have noticed that the fluid level in the oil rose higher than the fluid level in the water.

All right, what does that mean? It means that a greater volume of vegetable oil was necessary to counteract the gravitational force pulling down on the ball and washer than the volume of water necessary to accomplish the same thing. See Figure 3.13.

Figure 3.13

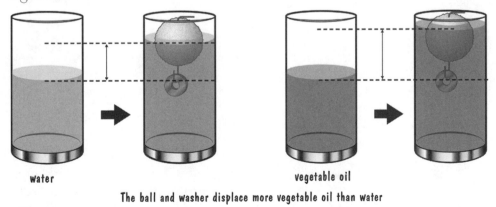

water   vegetable oil

The ball and washer displace more vegetable oil than water

---

[7] Here I'm ignoring the weight of the ball and paper clip, which isn't too bad an assumption as long as you have nice, heavy, metal washers.

Because vegetable oil and water have different densities (remember what density is?), the buoyant force must somehow depend on the density of the liquid into which you place a Styrofoam ball, or any other object. Yep, true. The buoyant force on an object immersed in a fluid depends not only on the amount of fluid displaced, but also on the density of the fluid. The denser the fluid, the greater the buoyant force. Although I haven't completely justified it, I hope I have made the following statement at least plausible.

> The upward buoyant force on an object is equal
> to the weight of fluid that the object displaces.

Think about that for a second. What that statement means is that the buoyant force really depends only on the fluid and not on the object, other than the fact that it's the object doing the displacing. Okay, so what's causing this upward force? To answer that, we take a look at what the molecules in the fluid are doing. What they're doing is moving around, bumping into one another and bumping into any object that might be submerged in the fluid. So, the fluid is exerting a force on any object submerged in it. Let's turn off gravity for a moment and see what would happen. As Figure 3.14 shows, larger submerged objects would have more fluid molecules hitting them.

Figure 3.14

Because the large object has more surface, more fluid molecules hit it. Gravity is "turned off" in this example.

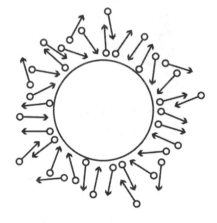

Figure 3.15

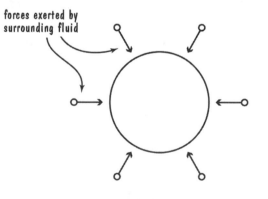

forces exerted by surrounding fluid

Because we're ignoring gravity, the forces exerted by the fluid on the object all cancel out.

Because we've turned off gravity (don't worry about floating away—we're just pretending), the objects get hit equally on all sides. The effect of the fluid molecules hitting the object from different directions cancels out, and there's no *net* force acting on the object (see Figure 3.15).

Of course, we can't turn off gravity. Gravity pulls down on the fluid (we call that the fluid's weight). Now think back to Chapter 1, where we found out that, because of the weight of a fluid, the pressure in the fluid increases with depth. That means more force per unit area the deeper you go. That means that the fluid molecules near the bottom of a submerged object push harder than the fluid molecules near the top of a submerged object. That leads to a net upward force! See Figure 3.16.

Figure 3.16

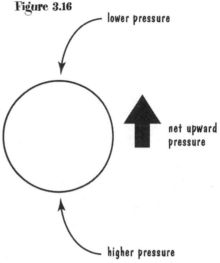

lower pressure

net upward pressure

higher pressure

Of course, denser fluids have more weight per unit volume, so the pressure in a fluid increases with depth faster for dense fluids than for less dense fluids.[8] And that's why the *weight* of the fluid is important.

And even more things to do before you read even more science stuff

Time to head back to the bathtub or kitchen sink. Actually, a large pan of water will do. Get a ball of modeling clay and drop it into the water to convince yourself that the ball sinks. Remove the ball of clay, and shape it into a boat, thinning it out and crimping up the sides to keep water out. This doesn't have to be a great-looking boat. What's in Figure 3.17 will do.

Check to see that the clay now floats in the water. If not, alter your design until you get it to float. That shouldn't take too much alteration.

Figure 3.17

---

[8] This is because of our relationship that tells how pressure in a fluid increases with depth. To remind you, that relationship is *Pressure at a depth h = pressure at the surface + pressure due to the weight of the water above the depth h.*

And even more science stuff

You've seen how something that is denser than water (clay) can float on water. How so? All you have to do is make sure the object displaces enough water so the buoyant force is as large as the force of gravity pulling the object down. Figure 3.18 shows what's happening when the clay is in the shape of a ball and when the clay is in the shape of a boat.

Figure 3.18

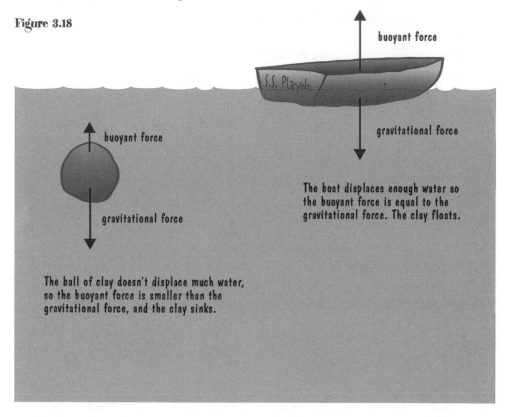

buoyant force

buoyant force

gravitational force

gravitational force

The boat displaces enough water so the buoyant force is equal to the gravitational force. The clay floats.

The ball of clay doesn't displace much water, so the buoyant force is smaller than the gravitational force, and the clay sinks.

So now you know how a steel ship can float on water, even though steel is pretty dense stuff.

To summarize, the whole issue of sinking and floating involves a balance between the force of gravity (an object's weight) and the buoyant force. If the buoyant force is equal to the object's weight, the object floats. If the buoyant force is less than the object's weight, the object sinks. If the buoyant force is larger than the object's weight, the object shoots upward. And of course, there are several ways to change the buoyant force.

As you move on to the summary and applications, I'm going to ask you to pay special attention to the applications involving air as a fluid. Those applications have a lot to do with the ideas about weather we'll get to later in the book.

Chapter Summary

- Density is a measure of how much "stuff" is contained in a given volume of an object or fluid. The more closely packed a substance is, the denser it is. The more the components of a substance weigh, the denser the substance. Mass density is the mass of a substance divided by the volume it occupies. Weight density is the weight of a substance divided by the volume it occupies. For the purposes of this book, we don't have to worry much about the distinction between mass density and weight density.

- Less dense fluids (both gas and liquid) float on top of denser fluids.

- Some fluids (both gas and liquid) are denser than other fluids. This depends on the components of the fluid, but can also depend on the fluid's temperature.

- All fluids (both gas and liquid) exert an upward buoyant force on objects partially or wholly submerged in them.

- Whether an object floats or sinks depends on the relative size of the object's weight and the buoyant force a fluid (either air or water or other fluid) exerts on it.

- The buoyant force exerted on an object is equal to the weight of the *fluid* displaced by the object.

- Buoyant forces owe their existence to the fact that fluids exert a greater pressure with increasing depth.

- Very dense substances can float on less dense substances providing they displace a sufficient amount of the less dense substance.

Applications

1. As we all know, hot air rises. But think about that for a second. Why in the world should hot air rise? Does it have a natural tendency to move away from the surface of the Earth? If you had a bunch of hot air molecules near the surface of the Earth, with no other air molecules around, would those hot air molecules just rise up all by themselves? Nope. The Earth's gravity pulls on everything, including hot air molecules, so they would stay near the Earth's surface. Here's the reality of the situation. Because they move faster and are able to create more space for themselves by pushing on surrounding air molecules, the molecules in a pocket of hot air expand and are less dense than the surrounding, cooler air molecules. Now we have a less dense fluid (remember, we consider air to be a fluid) sitting in a denser fluid (the cooler air). In effect, there is a buoyant force on the pocket of hot air that pushes it

up. Therefore, the hot air rises, not by itself, but because the surrounding cooler air pushes it upward.

2.   Because we're on the subject of hot air, let's talk about hot air balloons. First, they have "ballast" that consists of a bunch of heavy bags hanging over the side. These bags add weight, so the buoyant force on the balloon doesn't make it rise as fast as a helium balloon leaving a child's hand. To go higher, the balloon operator fires up a big ol' propane torch that heats the air inside the balloon. That makes the air inside the balloon less dense, decreasing the weight of the air inside the balloon, giving the advantage to the buoyant force of the surrounding air and leading to lift. Now you might be thinking that hot air balloons are made of cloth that won't expand forever, so how can the air inside become less dense? If so, you are ignoring the fact that hot air balloons have an escape route for the air inside, namely out the bottom of the balloon. As long as there's an escape route, the heated air inside can expand and become less dense. If the operator doesn't fire the torch, the air inside the balloon gradually cools, becomes denser, and the balloon sinks.

3.   Helium balloons rise upward. Why? Simply because a given volume of helium at a given pressure weighs less than the main components of air (nitrogen and oxygen) at that same volume and pressure, so the gas inside the balloon is less dense than the surrounding air. It's so much less dense that the helium plus balloon (the balloon itself weighs more than the surrounding air) is less dense than the surrounding air. A buoyant force pushes it up. I happen to live in the mountains, and when our kids get a helium balloon at lower altitude and bring it home, the balloon often doesn't float very well. The reason is that the atmosphere at higher altitudes is less dense than the atmosphere at lower altitudes (we covered that in Chapter 1). With less density, the air surrounding the balloon delivers a smaller upward buoyant force. And here you have to recall that the buoyant force depends on the *weight* of the surrounding fluid (air in this case), which depends on the density of the surrounding fluid.

4.   It's easier for a person to float in the ocean and in the Great Salt Lake than it is in a freshwater lake or a swimming pool. That's because saltwater is denser than freshwater. With a greater density, a given volume of saltwater weighs more than the same volume of freshwater. Because the buoyant force is equal to the weight of the fluid displaced, denser saltwater can exert a greater buoyant force than less dense freshwater.

5.   Submarines operate just about the same way that hot air balloons operate. By taking on or expelling water from ballast tanks, a submarine can change its weight. When a submarine changes its weight, that alters the relationship between the weight of the sub and the buoyant force pushing it up.

6. A popular science activity involves investigating what's known as a **Cartesian diver**. To make your own Cartesian diver, get an empty plastic 2-liter bottle and an eyedropper. Fill the bottle with water and then fill the eyedropper about half full of water. Drop the eyedropper into the bottle of water. If the dropper sinks, fish it out and put less water in the dropper. If the dropper floats, put the cap tightly on the bottle. Then squeeze the sides of the bottle. If you squeeze hard enough, the dropper will sink to the bottom. When you let go, the dropper rises to the top. How does this work? Just like a submarine. When you squeeze on the bottle, you increase the pressure of the water inside the bottle. That pushes water up into the dropper, making it heavier. If you increase the pressure enough, the dropper's weight overcomes the buoyant force and the dropper sinks. Look at Figure 3.19.

There are a couple of ways to analyze the Cartesian diver and, for that matter, a submarine. One way is to consider any water that goes up in the dropper as an addition to the weight of the dropper (that's what I did here). Another way is to consider that added water to still be a part of the surrounding water and not part of the dropper. In that case, what you are doing is decreasing the amount of water the dropper plus air displaces (the air inside compresses). That decreases the buoyant force while keeping the weight of the diver the same, with the same result—the dropper sinks. If you

Figure 3.19

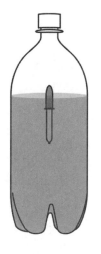
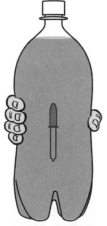

Squeezing the bottle forces more water into the eyedropper, making its weight larger than the buoyant force.

want to simplify the Cartesian diver, you can use a take-out packet of soy sauce in place of the eyedropper. When you squeeze the sides of the bottle, the packet will visibly contract as it sinks. In this case, the only proper explanation would be that the packet displaces less water, leading to a smaller buoyant force while the weight of the packet remains the same.

A Few Loose Ends

Before moving on to weather patterns, there are a few concepts about air and water we haven't covered. Some relate directly to weather and some don't, but given that most textbooks and curricula deal with these concepts, I figure I'd be letting you down if I left them out. Remember, this isn't just a book about weather. It's also about the properties of air and water, whether they apply to weather or not.

Daniel Bernoulli as a kid

"That's it?!! The water molecule lived happily ever after?!! What kind of story is that?! What about adhesion? And the equation of continuity? And what kind of molecules were they? Were they polar molecules?..."

4Chapter

Things to do before you read the science stuff

Figure 4.1

Fill a glass of water as close to the top as you can and make sure you're outside or right next to a sink. Then get an eyedropper and start adding drops of water to the glass one at a time. Watch from the side as you do this, and you should notice that at some point, the water bulges out over the top of the glass, but doesn't spill. If you're careful, you can get quite a water bulge before it finally spills over. Check out Figure 4.1.

Topic: properties of water

Go to: *www.scilinks.org*

Code: SFAWW11

Next get a bowl of water and sprinkle pepper over the surface of the water. Put a small drop of dishwashing soap on the edge of the bowl and see what happens. While you have the soap out, rub a bit on the edge of the glass you were using and then try again to get water to bulge over the edge of the glass by adding a drop at a time. Doesn't work very well, does it?

The science stuff

What you just observed has to do with a phenomenon known as **surface tension**. Nice term, but the term doesn't tell us what's going on. To get a better picture, we need to know what water molecules look like. They're composed of two hydrogen atoms and one oxygen atom. Because these three atoms share their electrons, and those negatively charged electrons spend more time around the oxygen atom than around the hydrogen atoms, the water molecule has one end that's positive and one end that's negative. Molecules that have one end positive and one negative are known as **polar molecules**. Check out Figure 4.2.

Figure 4.2

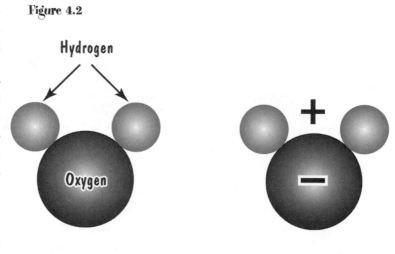

A water molecule is known as a polar molecule with one negative and one positive end.

Because plus and minus charges attract,[1] water molecules tend to hold on to one another. In the middle of a glass of water, each water molecule feels an attractive force from molecules all around it. The molecules on the surface of the water, however, get pulled back toward the rest of the water. See Figure 4.3.

The attraction is strong enough to cause surface tension. So, when you might expect water to spill over the edge of the glass, the attractive force of the other water molecules pulls the water at the edge back (Figure 4.4).

Figure 4.3

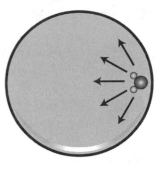

A water molecule surrounded by other water molecules is pulled in all directions.

A water molecule on the edge is pulled back toward the rest of the water.

Figure 4.4

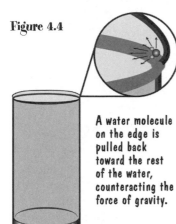

A water molecule on the edge is pulled back toward the rest of the water, counteracting the force of gravity.

Water's surface tension is what causes water to form into drops instead of some general blob. If gravity didn't exist, surface tension would cause water to form perfectly circular drops. Because gravity does exist, however, water forms that familiar look of a raindrop (Figure 4.5).

Okay, not quite. Drops that are just leaving your leaky water faucet might look like the drawing on the right in Figure 4.5, but falling raindrops don't look like that at all. The reason is that raindrops encounter air friction pushing up on them as they fall. If the drops are *really, really* small, then surface tension is the main force acting, and the raindrops are circular. For larger raindrops, the effect of surface tension is diminished in comparison to the air friction

Figure 4.5

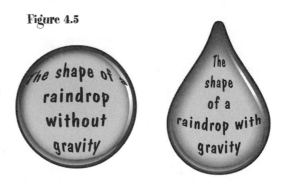

The shape of a raindrop without gravity

The shape of a raindrop with gravity

---

[1] For a whole lot more on this kind of interaction, see the *Stop Faking It!* book on Electricity and Magnetism.

Figure 4.6

The real shape of a raindrop

pushing upward. The effect of air friction pushing upward makes a falling raindrop look more like Figure 4.6.

Let's move on to what happened with the pepper on the bowl of water. When you sprinkle the pepper on the water, it stays on the surface because of the water's surface tension. The water molecules pulling on one another create sort of a "skin" on which the pepper rests instead of sinking. Now you add a drop of soap to one side of the water, and the pepper takes off. The reason is that when soap molecules come in contact with water molecules, the soap molecules tend to grab onto the water molecules and keep them from pulling on one another. So, you remove the effects of surface tension at one end of the bowl of water by adding soap. The rest of the water in the bowl retains its surface tension and pulls back away from the drop of soap. The pepper goes along for the ride.

More things to do before you read more science stuff

Dip the edge of a coffee filter into a glass or bowl of water. Water will creep up the side of the filter. If you wait long enough, the entire filter will get wet. Why does the water go against the force of gravity and move upward?

Look from the side at a clear glass half full of water. At the surface of the water, you should notice that the level of the water is slightly higher at the edges (next to the glass) than at the center, as in Figure 4.7. How come?

Figure 4.7

The next time you're having Cheerios for breakfast, drop two dry Cheerios into a bowl of milk. The two Cheerios move together, almost as if they have some kind of innate attraction. If you don't have any Cheerios in the house, place two dry straws or dry pencils near each other in a pan or bowl of water. They should do the same thing the Cheerios did.

More science stuff

Water molecules, being polar molecules, tend to attract one another. This happens because the molecules align themselves so the plus sides and the minus sides are together and the pluses and minuses attract.[2] The polar nature of water mol-

---

[2] To fully understand this attraction, you have to know a few things about electric forces. See the *Stop Faking It!* book on Electricity and Magnetism for more detail.

ecules also makes them attracted to other materials. For the record, this attraction to other substances is known as **adhesion**. Always nice to have another vocabulary word. When you dip a coffee filter into a glass of water, the water molecules in the glass are attracted to the molecules in the paper, and they sort of climb aboard. As they do this, they bring other water molecules with them.[3] Eventually, the entire coffee filter gets wet.

The same thing is going on with a glass half full of water. The water molecules near the inside surface of the glass are attracted to the glass to the point that they "climb up" the sides a bit. Of course, they bring other molecules with them, leading to the shape you see (Figure 4.8).

Figure 4.8

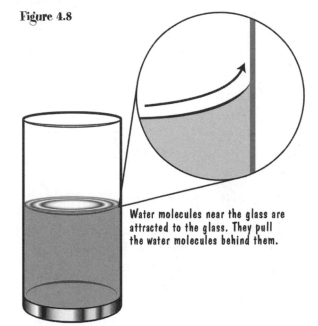

Water molecules near the glass are attracted to the glass. They pull the water molecules behind them.

Finally, we have Cheerios. Same process. The water molecules, in addition to being attracted to one another, are also attracted to the Cheerios. This results in the Cheerios coming together (see Figure 4.9).

Figure 4.9

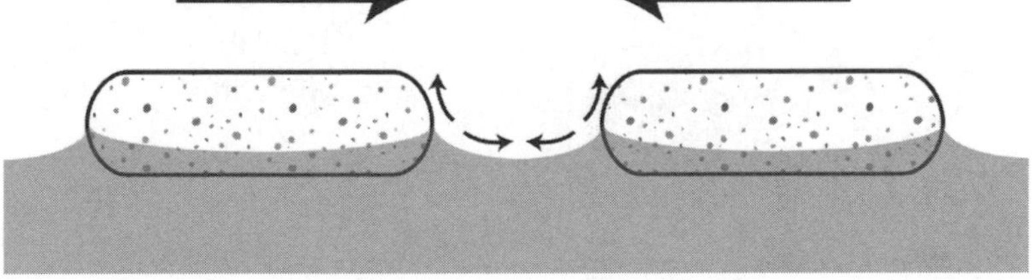

The attraction of the water molecules to the Cheerios (adhesion) and to one another results in the Cheerios coming together.

---

[3] Even though the "lead" water molecules are more attracted to the coffee filter than they are the other water molecules, there still is an attraction between neighboring water molecules.

Even more things to do before you read even more science stuff

Get an empty 2-liter plastic bottle with a screw-on cap. Remove the cap and use a nail to poke a hole in the center of the cap. The easiest way to do this is to take the cap outside, place it on the ground, and hammer the nail through the center of the cap. If you do this on the Formica counter in the kitchen, you will have a chip in that counter that will serve as a constant reminder to your spouse of your stupidity. Yep, I did it, but I wasn't stupid enough to hammer a nail into the counter. I used an electric drill.

Fill the bottle with water, leaving the cap off. Go outside and squeeze the bottle. Note how fast the water comes out. Refill the bottle with water and put the cap with the hole in it on the bottle. Head back outside and squeeze the bottle again. Yes, you too can create your own Super Soaker.

Even more science stuff

In order for you to understand what just happened, I have to remind you that liquids are not compressible, at least not to any appreciable extent. Gases you can compress, but not liquids. Therefore, if you push on one side of a liquid, the liquid molecules in between will transfer that push all the way to the other side of the liquid.

Topic: fluids and pressure

Go to: *www.scilinks.org*

Code: SFAWW12

A crowd of closely packed people behaves a lot like a liquid. If the people are packed into a room and are standing right next to one another, with no room in between, then a push on one side of the room will make its way to the other side of the room. See Figure 4.10.

Now, let's suppose there are lots and lots of people waiting to get into a rock concert. There's a big crowd that has to pass through a couple of turnstiles, meaning that the crowd must narrow down considerably. We know what would happen if the people at the back be-

Figure 4.10

A shove here. . .

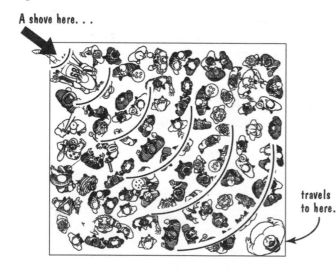

travels to here.

gan shoving toward the front. The people at the turnstiles would be crushed! But let's suppose we have covered these people in vegetable oil, and they're really slippery and able to slide over and across one another with little trouble. In other words, they won't get hung up on any railings or the turnstiles. In this situation, when people at the back start pushing, the people up front will simply begin moving through the turnstiles much, much faster than they were before. If those people up front move fast enough, no one will bunch up, and the crowd will move smoothly through the turnstiles, as in Figure 4.11.

Well, it turns out that water molecules behave a whole lot like slippery humans. Although these molecules do get hung up on the sides of a container, they mostly just slip and slide over and across one another and along the sides of the container. When you squeeze on a 2-liter bottle that has a small hole in the cap, the water molecules near the cap speed up dramatically so they make it through the opening without causing the molecules behind them to bunch up (Figure 4.12).

In fact, there's a mathematical relationship that tells just how much the water speeds up in going from a large cross-sectional area to a small cross-sectional area. Here it is:

$$A_1 v_1 = A_2 v_2$$

where A_1 is the cross-sectional area at point 1, v_1 is the velocity of the water at point 1, A_2 is the cross-sectional area at point 2, and

Figure 4.11

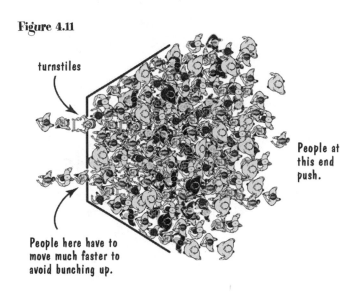

turnstiles

People at this end push.

People here have to move much faster to avoid bunching up.

Figure 4.12

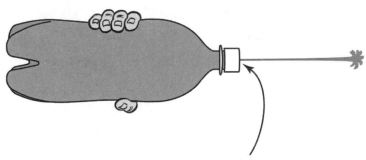

Water molecules at the small opening speed up in response to pressure from other water molecules in the bottle.

Chapter

v_2 is the velocity of the water at point 2. Figure 4.13 illustrates the situation.

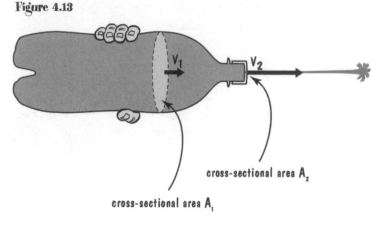

Figure 4.13

So, when water (or any other fluid for that matter) goes from a large cross-sectional area to a small cross-sectional area (A gets smaller), the velocity of the water increases (v gets larger). Of course,

cross-sectional area A_2

cross-sectional area A_1

the reverse holds true. If a fluid goes from a small cross-sectional area to a large one, the velocity of the fluid decreases. We can illustrate this with a teeter-totter that represents the mathematical relationship, as in Figure 4.14. And for the record, the relationship $A_1v_1 = A_2v_2$ is known as the **equation of continuity**.[4]

Figure 4.14

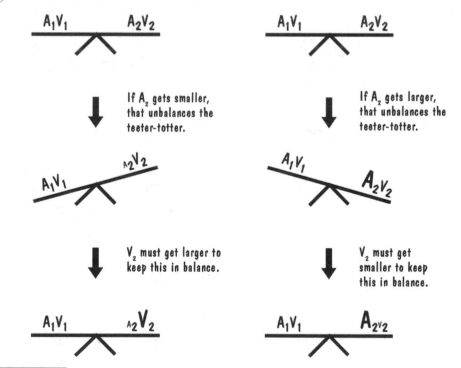

---

[4] Actually, this is a special case of the equation of continuity, where the density of the fluid does not change. That's what we're dealing with here, so no big deal.

Before moving on, I should tell you that there are several assumptions we make when applying the equation of continuity. One is that the fluid we're dealing with is not *viscous*. You can think of viscosity as a measure of the fluid's "stickiness." Oil is a highly viscous fluid and water has a low viscosity. Another assumption is that the liquid flows smoothly without any rotational flow that would disrupt the motion of the fluid. Finally, we assume that the velocity of the fluid at any point doesn't change over a given period of time. These assumptions are sometimes pretty good, and sometimes not so good, but they illustrate something about scientific models of how things behave. The models are good only so long as our assumptions are close to correct. The best way to make the assumptions good is to perform controlled experiments. The best way to make sure the assumptions will fall apart is to apply them to everyday experiences! Hopefully you'll see what I'm talking about when we get into describing weather patterns. We might understand various processes that cause weather, but when we put all those processes together in an attempt to understand everything that's happening in global weather, we can often go wrong. So, give those weather forecasters a break!

Okay, that's all I'm going to cover in this chapter. I know the ideas are a bit disjointed, but I also told you we were tying together a few loose ends in order to help you should you come across these ideas when you have to teach students how air and water behave.

Chapter Summary

- Some liquids have a sort of "skin" on their surface, known as surface tension. Surface tension is caused by the attraction of the molecules of the liquid for one another. Liquids that are composed of polar molecules, such as water, exhibit surface tension.

- The polar nature of some liquid molecules leads to adhesion, which is the attraction of a liquid for a different substance. Water is a liquid that exhibits strong adhesion properties.

- When fluids (both gases and liquids) move from one cross-sectional area to another, they tend to change speeds. This change in speed is governed by the "equation of continuity," which applies better to liquids than to gases.

Applications

1. In the Applications section of Chapter 2, I had you do a magic trick in which you place an index card over a full glass and turn the glass upside down. The card stays in place. The reason the card stays in place has a lot to

do with differences in air pressure, but it also has to do with surface tension and adhesion. The adhesion of the water for the card and the surface tension between water molecules helps keep the card in place (Figure 4.15). To see that surface tension is important, rub soap around the rim of the glass before you try the trick. That significantly reduces the surface tension of the water there, and the trick just won't work.

Okay, one more demonstration that surface tension is at work. Replace the index card with a fine, wire mesh screen. The trick still works because the surface tension of the water inside each hole in the screen is strong enough to hold everything together.

2. Next time you're around a slow-moving river or creek, or even a lake, look closely near the shore around sundown (you know, when the bugs come out). Without much trouble, you see bugs known as "water striders," which skim along the surface of the water. What's holding them up? The surface tension of the water. Look closely and you'll see that the water has small depressions where the water striders' legs touch the water. To create your own version of a water strider, fill a glass to the rim with water. Then take a paper clip and ease it onto the water from the side of the glass (Figure 4.16). If you're careful in doing this, you can get the

Figure 4.15

The surface tension of the water and the adhesion between the water and the card help hold the card in place.

Figure 4.16

Ease the paper clip onto the water from the side.

paper clip to float on the water due to the water's surface tension. Add a drop of soap and the paper clip will sink.

3. In case you think that soap is only good for ruining surface tension, grab a bottle of bubble solution and blow a few bubbles. The reason these things form into bubbles is that soap molecules have a surface tension of their own. It's not as large as the surface tension of water, but it's enough to keep a soap bubble together.

4. The attraction that many fluid molecules have for other surfaces is the mechanism behind what's known as **paper chromatography**. In this procedure, you place a dot of some substance on porous paper (like a coffee filter) and then dip the paper in a liquid. As the liquid climbs up the paper (due to adhesion), it encounters the dot of substance, which tends to dissolve in the fluid. As the fluid continues to climb up the paper, the components of the substance separate according to their

Topic: chromatography

Go to: *www.scilinks.org*

Code: SFAWW13

mass. This helps you identify what the substance contains. This is one way to identify the components of a blood sample. To see a crude version of this, put a dot of black, washable marker on a coffee filter and dip the bottom of the filter in water. As the water climbs up the filter, the component colors of the black marker will separate. Very pretty!

5. I mentioned Super Soakers in this chapter. Let's look a bit closer at how they work. First, there's a small opening through which the water squirts. The equation $A_1 v_1 = A_2 v_2$ tells us that any water forced through this opening (small value of A) will be moving quickly (large v). But how do you force water out of the opening? By increasing the air pressure inside the container of water, that's how. As you pump a Super Soaker, you add more and more air molecules to the chamber. More molecules means an increase in pressure.

Small-Scale Weather

Finally we get to applying the concepts covered so far to the Earth's weather. In this chapter, I'm going to deal with a number of basic mechanisms that govern small-scale things such as cloud formation, rain, fog, and the like. Now it might not seem like a small-scale issue when you're getting rained on or are shoveling a foot of snow from your driveway, but compared to weather on the Earth as a whole, such things *are* small scale. In the next chapter, I'll cover large-scale weather patterns such as large high and low pressure areas, storm fronts, and the movement of weather systems across the Earth.

"My bunion's achin', Pa. It must be gonna rain."

Things to do before you read the science stuff

Run your hand under a water faucet and then wave it (your hand, not the faucet) in the air. How does this make your hand feel? Cooler, right? Now substitute rubbing alcohol for the water and wave your hand in the air again. Any difference in how your hand feels compared to when you used water?

Head to the refrigerator in your house. Notice the temperature right behind the refrigerator compared to the temperature in your house as a whole. Okay, that's it. Time to learn something.

The science stuff

It probably won't come as any surprise to you that when you wave a wet hand in the air, the water on your hand evaporates, or changes from a liquid (water) to a gas (water vapor). **Evaporation** of water happens all around us, so it's pretty common. Let's take a closer look at what's going

SCiLINKS.
THE WORLD'S A CLICK AWAY
Topic: evaporation
Go to: *www.scilinks.org*
Code: SFAWW14

on in evaporation. In a liquid state, water molecules are relatively close together and, as we saw with surface tension, they exert forces on one another. When these water molecules become water vapor, they are on average a whole lot farther apart than when they're a liquid, and they don't exert any appreciable forces on one another unless they collide. You might want to think back to our model of gases as a collection of people bumping into one another. So, in changing water from a liquid to a gas, the molecules must be pulled apart. That takes energy. In the case of your wet hand, that energy is in the form of **heat** transferred from your hand to the water. See Figure 5.1.

Figure 5.1

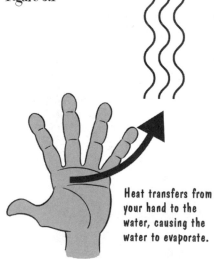

Heat transfers from your hand to the water, causing the water to evaporate.

Evaporation of water, therefore, involves water *gaining* energy at the expense of its surroundings. When you substitute rubbing alcohol for water, your hand feels even cooler than with the water. That's because the molecules in alcohol are more volatile, meaning they evaporate (break apart) more easily than water molecules. When the alcohol evaporates from your hand, heat transfers from your hand to the liquid more quickly than with water. A quicker transfer of heat means your hand cools off faster.

That's one **change of state** out of the way (liquid to gas). What about going from a solid to a liquid? To figure out what's going on there, just consider what happens when you put ice cubes in a glass of hot water. The ice melts and the water gets cooler. That means that the ice (a solid) absorbs heat from the water as it melts. So, changing from a solid to a liquid or a liquid to a gas requires energy, usually in the form of a heat transfer.

Okay, what was it like behind the refrigerator? Warm, huh? That means the refrigerator is giving off heat as it does its job. The job of a refrigerator is to make things colder. More importantly for our purposes, refrigerators have a freezer section that turns water into ice. Just as ice absorbs heat in going from a solid to a liquid, water gives off heat in going from a liquid to a solid.[1] Also, even though we haven't demonstrated it, water vapor gives off heat when it goes from a gas (the vapor) to a liquid (water). If you want fancy names for the heat given off or absorbed when there's a change of state, it's called the **latent heat of fusion** when something goes from a solid to a liquid (and vice versa) and the **latent heat of vaporization** when something goes from a liquid to a gas (or vice versa).

So what does all this have to do with weather? A lot. The energy that fuels thunderstorms and even hurricanes comes from the evaporation and subsequent **condensation** (water going from a gas to a liquid) taking place in those storms. More on that in Chapter 7.

Since we're on the subject of evaporation and condensation, I'll take a moment and explain humidity and relative humidity. **Humidity** is simply a measure of the amount of water vapor in the air. The more water vapor, the more humid it is. At a given temperature, however, there is only so much water vapor that can be in the air. If you get more than this "saturation level," then ex-

Topic: What is heat?
Go to: *www.scilinks.org*
Code: SFAWW15

Topic: heat transfer
Go to: *www.scilinks.org*
Code: SFAWW16

Topic: changes of state
Go to: *www.scilinks.org*
Code: SFAWW17

Figure 5.2

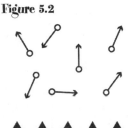
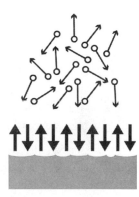

The air is not saturated. More water molecules are becoming water vapor than water vapor is condensing to form water.

The air is saturated with water vapor. For each water molecule that becomes water vapor, a molecule of water vapor is condensing to form liquid water.

[1] So you don't get the wrong idea, the warm air at the back of a refrigerator doesn't come directly from the heat released as water becomes ice. There are various heat transfers in between.

cess water vapor simply condenses into water at the same rate that water might be evaporating into water vapor. One way of thinking of this saturation level is that the air simply can't "hold" any more water vapor than a certain amount. See Figure 5.2.

This brings us to **relative humidity**, which is the actual amount of water vapor in the air divided by the amount of water vapor in the air if it's saturated.

$$relative\ humidity = \frac{amount\ of\ water\ vapor\ actually\ in\ the\ air}{amount\ of\ water\ vapor\ in\ the\ air\ when\ it's\ saturated} \times 100\%$$

Because the actual amount of water vapor in the air can't be greater than the amount the air can hold when it's saturated, relative humidity is a number between 0 and 100%. Dry air has a relative humidity around 15% and humid air can have a relative humidity of 90% or higher. Of course, temperature has an effect on the amount of moisture air can "hold." In general, hotter air can handle more water vapor than cooler air. That's why a relative humidity of 80% is a whole lot more uncomfortable in summer than in winter.

More things to do before you read more science stuff

We've been using the word *temperature* quite a bit, but we haven't really defined it. Think for a moment about temperature differences you encounter everyday. You touch a warm cup of coffee and your hand heats up. You put your hand in cold water, and your hand gets cooler. Unless you live in Hawaii or some other tropical paradise, you spend much of winter trying to maintain a temperature difference between the inside of your home and the outside. Think back to our model of what air molecules are doing (you know, people walking around bouncing into one another and the walls of their container) when they're hot or when they're cold.

While you're thinking of that, get a glass of hot water and a glass of cold water. Put a drop of food coloring in each and watch what happens. Notice any difference in how fast the food coloring spreads out? Does that tell you something about what hot and cold liquid molecules are doing?

All right, let's do something a bit different. Get an empty saucepan and place it on the stove. Touch the side of the pan to note its temperature. Then turn on the heating element (electric or gas) under the saucepan and touch the side of the pan (not the insulated handle!) every 10 seconds or so to get an idea of how fast the pan is heating up. Of course, you need to be careful about this. Once the pan gets almost too hot to touch, turn off the stove. No sense burning yourself or ruining the saucepan.

Cool down the saucepan by running it under cold water and then fill the pan with water. Return to the stove and start heating up the pan of water. This time, touch the water every 10 seconds or so to get an idea of how fast the *water* is heating up. Again, be careful. Even though a watched pot never boils, that's just a saying. Don't get a third-degree burn and then tell the doctor you were only following instructions in a stupid book.

More science stuff

Let's start with the food coloring in the hot and cold water. In the hot water, the food coloring spreads out faster than in the cold water. One explanation for that—the one we're going to use—is that the water molecules in hot water are moving around faster than the water molecules in the cold water. This faster movement causes the food coloring to spread out faster as it gets jostled around by the water molecules. So, we might expect that temperature has a lot to do with the speed of the molecules. Higher average speeds mean higher temperatures and lower average speeds mean lower temperatures.[2]

The situation is the same with a gas, such as the air. The average speed of air molecules is higher for hot air than it is for cool air. That makes sense, because if the air feels cool to you, those molecules aren't hitting you as hard (they're moving slower) as the molecules in hot air. That results in a transfer of energy (heat) from you to the cool air molecules. Similarly, when faster moving hot air molecules hit you, they transfer energy (in the form of heat) *to* your body. See Figure 5.3.

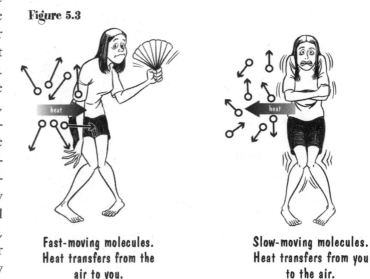

Figure 5.3

Fast-moving molecules. Heat transfers from the air to you.

Slow-moving molecules. Heat transfers from you to the air.

---

[2] Note that I'm using the word *average*. It's impossible for us to keep track of the speeds of individual molecules. Some are moving much faster than the average speed and some much slower, but as long as the temperature in the liquid is uniform, the liquid acts as if all of the molecules are moving at the average speed.

Just so we get things technically correct, the temperature of a gas is defined as the *average kinetic energy* of the molecules in the gas. I'm not going to go into a detailed discussion of kinetic energy,[3] so it's okay if, for now, you simply have the notion of higher temperatures meaning higher average speeds of the molecules involved, whether we're talking about solids or liquids or gases.

Now that we have a better picture of what temperature is, let's return to the concepts of humidity and relative humidity. The higher the temperature of the air, the more water vapor the air can hold. That makes sense because air molecules and water vapor molecules are moving faster at higher temperatures. The faster the water vapor molecules move, the less likely they are to condense into liquid water. If air can hold more water vapor at higher temperatures, that means the humidity saturation level is different at different temperatures. If the saturation level is different at different temperatures, then relative humidity means different things at different temperatures. Let's look at an example. Suppose it's 60 degrees Fahrenheit outside and the relative humidity is 100%. That means the air is saturated with water vapor. Now suppose the Sun comes out and the air heats up to around 80 degrees Fahrenheit without any water vapor being added to or removed from the air. Because the temperature increases, the saturation level of the air increases. The actual amount of water vapor in the air hasn't changed, though, so the *relative* humidity goes way down. In this example, the relative humidity will decrease to around 50%. What's the point? Well, relative humidity says a lot about chances for precipitation (rain, snow, etc.). The higher the relative humidity, the greater the chance that water vapor will condense into rain or snow. Therefore, as long as the outside temperature increases during the day, you have less chance of precipitation because the relative humidity probably is decreasing. If the temperature stays the same or even decreases, you have a much greater chance of precipitation because the relative humidity increases.[4]

Now let's move on to the heating of an empty pan versus the heating of a pan of water. You should have noticed that an empty pan heats up much quicker than a pan of water. If you want to take the time, you will also find out that a hot

---

[3] See the *Stop Faking It!* book on Energy for a complete treatment of kinetic energy. For that matter, my whole discussion of heat transfer, temperature, and change of state is pretty brief here. You'll get a much better understanding of these concepts by taking a look at the Energy book.

---

[4] As I told you earlier, actual weather patterns can be complicated, and simple rules seldom work in all cases. Here I have implied that if the relative humidity is high but the temperature rises, then you won't get rain, and if the temperature decreases, you will get rain or snow. That would be true if relative humidity were the only thing that determined whether or not it rains. As you'll see later in the book, patterns of rising and sinking air have a whole lot to do with precipitation, so relative humidity alone doesn't give you the entire picture.

empty pan also *cools down* much faster than a pan of hot water. This is generally true of all solids when compared to water. To be more specific, for a given amount of heat transferred, solids change their temperature more rapidly than does water. So, if you add a certain amount of heat to a solid, the solid will have a larger rise in temperature than a body of water that is exposed to the same amount of heat.[5]

What does a pan of water have to do with the weather? I'll give you one example. If you live near the ocean, you might notice that, during relatively good weather, there often is a breeze blowing from the ocean toward the land during the day and a breeze blowing from the land toward the ocean at night. These breezes are due to the changes in temperature of the land and the ocean during the day and night. In the daytime, the sun heats up both the land and the ocean. Because the land undergoes a greater temperature change with this heat input than the water does, the land becomes much warmer than the water (think about how hot that beach sand is compared to the water on a summer day). The air above the warmer land heats up. As the air above land warms up, it pushes harder on the surrounding air and becomes less dense. The cooler and denser air over the ocean then pushes that warm air up, and in the process creates a wind from ocean toward land.

When the sun goes down, both the ocean and the land cool off. The land cools off much faster than the ocean, though, and we end up with the land being cooler than the ocean (at night the sand on a beach is

Figure 5.4

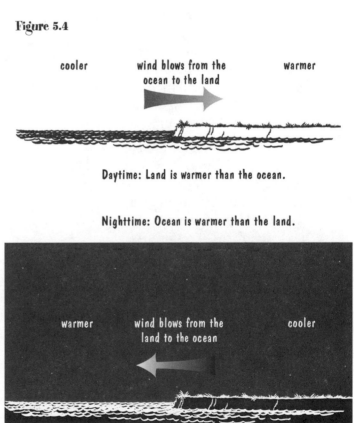

Daytime: Land is warmer than the ocean.

Nighttime: Ocean is warmer than the land.

---

[5] Again, see the Energy book for much more detail, and even an equation (woo hoo!) that describes the process.

cooler than the ocean water). Once again, the air above the land and the ocean changes temperature accordingly. At night, we end up with the air over the ocean being warmer than the air over the land. This is the reverse of the previous situation, and we get a breeze from the land toward the ocean. Figure 5.4 shows how all this works.

To keep things in perspective, the winds blowing in or out near an ocean are an example of small-scale weather. Local winds don't have a lot to do with major patterns of weather across the Earth.

Even more things to do before you read even more science stuff

Get a 2-liter plastic bottle, a small votive candle, and something that gives off smoke, such as incense or a cigarette. Cut the bottom off the 2-liter bottle and then cut a rectangular opening in the side, as shown in Figure 5.5.

Set the bottle on a table with the cap off as shown in Figure 5.6. Place the candle inside the bottle and light it. Then hold your smoking object near the rectangular opening and notice what the smoke does.

Even more science stuff

You should have noticed that the smoke moved from outside the bottle, through the opening, up inside the bottle, and then back down the outside of the bottle. In other words, the path of the smoke

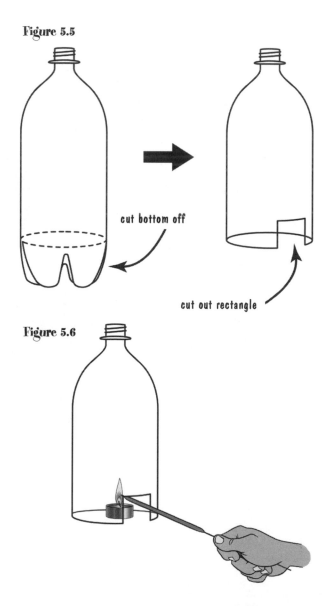

Figure 5.5

cut bottom off

cut out rectangle

Figure 5.6

Figure 5.7

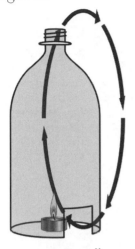

a convection cell

looked like that shown in Figure 5.7. A pattern of circulation of air like this is known as a **convection cell**.

First I'll give you the wrong explanation of what's going on. This wrong explanation is all over the place, in many textbooks and resource books, and even in otherwise accurate resource books. The explanation is that the candle heats the air above it. This hot air rises, and cooler air from outside the bottle rushes in to take its place. As the hot air rises in the bottle, it cools and eventually sinks back down on the outside of the bottle.

Now for the correct explanation. As I discussed in the Applications section of Chapter 3, hot air does not rise all by itself. If you had a big bunch of hot air near the surface of the Earth, with no other air around it, would the hot air rise up? Nope. Gravity acts on this hot air just as it acts on everything else, so the hot air would stay where it is. The hot air right above the candle *is*, however, less dense than the cooler air outside the bottle (it's less dense because it pushes harder on the air around it, creating more room for itself). Therefore, the buoyant force exerted by the denser, cooler air around it pushes the hot air upwards. The cooler air doing the pushing then gets heated by the candle and in turn gets pushed upward by more cool air. It *is* true that as the hot air rises it cools and eventually sinks down on the outside of the bottle, creating the convection cell. See Figure 5.8.

Figure 5.8

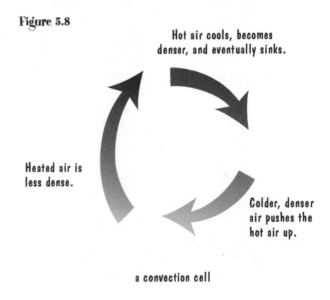

Hot air cools, becomes denser, and eventually sinks.

Heated air is less dense.

Colder, denser air pushes the hot air up.

a convection cell

Convection cells are involved in both small-scale and large-scale weather. In small-scale weather, convection cells describe what's happening in a thunderstorm. In large-scale weather, convection cells account for the fact that we have major desert areas and tropical regions. More on that in the next chapter.

One thing I can address right now is the fact that when hot air rises (pushed up by cooler surrounding air), it cools.[6] A pocket of hot air has molecules that are, on average, moving faster than the surrounding air molecules. Because they're moving faster than their surroundings, they push harder than the surrounding molecules and create more space for themselves, causing the hot air to expand. When the hot air molecules push on surrounding molecules, they transfer energy to the slower moving molecules. This transfer of energy means the hot air molecules slow down. When they slow down, they end up with a lower temperature. In other words, the air cools. Check out Figure 5.9.

Figure 5.9

As the hot air rises, it pushes on the surrounding air and loses energy. As a result, the molecules move slower and you have cooler air.

A pocket of hot air is pushed upward by surrounding cold air.

And even more things to do before you read even more science stuff

For this next activity, you need a fresh, empty 2-liter plastic bottle with lid, a few wooden matches, and a flashlight. Remove the label on the bottle and position the flashlight so it shines through the bottle. Either that or have a friend hold the flashlight. Put a small bit of warm water in the bottle and put the lid on. Do you see anything happening inside the bottle? Try squeezing and then releasing the sides of the bottle. Any change? Don't spend too much time looking for something to happen, because it's not likely that anything *will* happen!

Take the lid off the bottle. Then strike one of the matches, blow it out, and let the resulting smoke enter the bottle. You can even drop the match into the

---

[6] I don't mean to imply that only hot air cools as it rises. *Hot* is a relative term. As long as a pocket of air is warmer than the surrounding air, that pocket will be pushed upward and will cool in the process.

bottom of the bottle. If there's a fair amount of smoke in the bottle, then put the lid on. Otherwise, strike a second match, blow it out, and use it as a source for more smoke inside the bottle. Once you have smoke in the bottle, put the lid on and shine the flashlight through the bottle. Squeeze the sides of the bottle. What happens? Release the sides and look for a change. Keep squeezing and releasing to convince yourself that the "cloud" you made inside the bottle disappears and reappears depending on how hard you squeeze the bottle.

And even more science stuff

I'll start out with a generic explanation of how clouds form, and then I'll address what happened in your 2-liter bottle and why that is closer to what really happens when clouds form. The generic explanation is that warm, humid air rises, pushed upward by surrounding cooler air. As that warm, humid air cools (remember that warm air cools as it rises), it gets cold enough for the water vapor in the air to condense into tiny water droplets, which make up clouds.

Without any smoke in your 2-liter bottle, you most likely didn't get any clouds. But shouldn't you get clouds? After all, you have water vapor evaporating from the warm water at the bottom of the bottle. As this air rises and comes in contact with the cool sides of the bottle, the air cools. With cooler air, shouldn't the water vapor condense into water droplet? Well yes, and you might even see a bit of condensation on the sides of the bottle. You don't see clouds, though, because for water vapor to condense into water droplets, the molecules of water vapor not only have to collide, they have to hang onto one another. With fast-moving molecules, it's just not all that likely that the colliding molecules stick together. Result: no clouds.

Now we introduce smoke particles. These smoke particles give the molecules of water vapor something to hold onto, resulting in the water vapor condensing into water droplets, and a cloud. Small particles such as the particles of smoke are known as **condensation nuclei**. In general, water vapor needs condensation nuclei in order for clouds to form. In real life, these condensation nuclei can be smoke, salt in the air (near the ocean), dust, or even pollution.

When you squeeze the bottle, the clouds inside disappear. That's because by squeezing the bottle you are increasing the pressure inside. Increasing the pressure causes the molecules in the bottle (both air molecules and water vapor molecules) to move faster. When they move faster, the tiny water droplets that formed the cloud again become water vapor. When you release the bottle, the pressure inside decreases again, and a cloud forms. This also corresponds to what happens in real life. Even if you have lots of water vapor in the air, clouds are unlikely to form if the air pressure is high. Clouds are much more likely to form in areas of low air pressure. Of course, we haven't yet covered the issue of high and low pressure areas on the Earth. I guess you'll have to wait until the next chapter to see what's going on.

You now have a pretty good idea of how clouds form and how that condensation might result in water droplets large enough to result in rain. What about snow? Well, it's mostly a matter of temperature. As a condensed water droplet rises it can possibly cool enough to freeze into an ice crystal. If the air this crystal encounters as it moves up gets colder than about 5 degrees Fahrenheit, then the crystal grows six arms (the number of arms has everything to do with the structure of ice crystals) and begins to look like what you normally think of as a snowflake. As this crystal gets heavy enough to fall, it changes even more so it does become a snowflake. As long as the air between where the crystal forms and the ground is cool enough, the crystal will survive as snow. Otherwise it melts on the way down and you have rain.

Chapter Summary

- When substances change state (from solid to liquid, from liquid to solid, and then back again), a transfer of energy in the form of heat is involved. Adding heat to a solid can cause it to go from a solid to a liquid, and adding heat to a liquid can cause it to go from a liquid to a gas. When a substance goes from a gas to a liquid to a solid, there is a release of heat.

- Temperature is an indication of the speed at which the molecules of a substance are moving (on average). Higher temperatures mean faster speeds, and lower temperatures mean slower speeds.

- Humidity is a measure of the amount of water vapor in the air.

- Relative humidity is the amount of water vapor in the air divided by the amount of water vapor in the air when the air is saturated.

- Relative humidity changes with changes in temperature. When the temperature increases while the amount of water vapor in the air remains constant, the relative humidity decreases. When the temperature decreases while the amount of water vapor in the air remains constant, the relative humidity increases. These relationships have everything to do with the fact that warm air holds more molecules of water vapor (prior to those molecules condensing into rain) than does cool air.

- Solids generally undergo a greater change in temperature for a given input or output of heat than do liquids.

- Whenever fluids (both air and water) of different density come in contact, the denser fluid pushes the less dense fluid upward. As the less dense substance cools as it rises, its density increases and it sinks. This air then tends to push other, less dense air upward. This arrangement is known as a convection cell.

● Hot air does not rise all by itself. Generally, it is pushed up by colder, less dense, air.

Applications

1. An instrument that measures the humidity of the air is known as a **hygrometer**. I'll bet you'd just love to make your own hygrometer, huh? To do that, get an empty toilet-paper tube, a couple of pushpins, an emery board (used for filing your nails), and a nice, long strand of human hair. Use a pushpin to poke holes in each end of the emery board. Then put the two pushpins into the toilet-paper tube as shown in Figure 5.10. The emery board should be between the pushpin and the tube at the bottom.

Now tie one end of the human hair to the push pin at the bottom, place it up and around the top pushpin, and then tie it through the free hole in the end of the emery board. Before you tie that last knot, adjust the length of the hair until you have something like Figure 5.11.

To see that this contraption measures humidity, take it from a regular room into the bathroom and turn the shower on hot so you get lots of steam. The emery board should

Figure 5.10

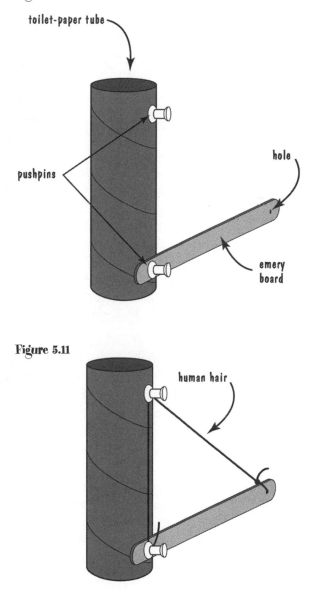

Figure 5.11

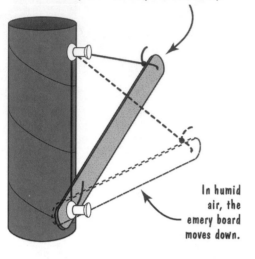

Figure 5.12

In dry air, the emery board moves up.

In humid air, the emery board moves down.

change position, as shown in Figure 5.12.

To use your human-hair hygrometer, place it somewhere it's protected from the wind, and watch the emery board move up and down as the humidity of the atmosphere changes. How does it work, you ask? Human hair absorbs and releases water as the humidity changes. As the humidity increases, the hair absorbs more water and, as a result, increases in length. When the hair gives off water and becomes drier, the hair decreases in length. The changes in length of the hair cause the emery board to move up and down. Now, the fact that human hair absorbs and releases water explains why you are more likely to have a bad hair day when the humidity is high.

2. If you live in an area where the humidity reaches high levels, you undoubtedly know that high humidity is much more uncomfortable in the summer than it is in the winter. The reason is that we humans sweat in order to cool off. When the sweat evaporates, it takes heat from your body and cools you off. If the relative humidity is high, though, that means the air around you is already close to its saturation point. Therefore, for every bit of water that evaporates from your skin, just as much water vapor from the air condenses on your skin. Overall, there is very little cooling and you feel uncomfortable. High relative humidity in the winter isn't such a big deal, because with the temperature being cooler, you don't need to cool off through the evaporation of sweat.

3. I already talked about ocean breezes that blow from ocean to land during the day and from land to the ocean at night. A similar effect happens on mountainsides. During the day, you often get an updraft (winds blowing up the mountainside), followed by a downdraft (winds blowing down the mountainside) at night. This is due to the fact that a mountain has mainly rocks and bare ground at higher elevations and mainly trees at lower elevations. For a given input of heat, the rocks and bare ground change temperature faster than the trees. So, during the day the rocks and bare ground at the top of the mountain become hotter than the trees at the bottom. This makes the air at the top of the mountain hotter than the air at the bottom. The cooler air pushes the warmer air upward, resulting in a breeze blowing up the mountainside. At night, the rocks and bare ground cool off faster than the trees, reversing the location of warm and cool air. The winds blow

down the mountainside because the cooler air up high is denser than the warmer air below. Figure 5.13 illustrates this process.

Figure 5.13

During the day, the top of the mountain heats up faster than the forested land below. This causes wind to blow up the mountainside.

At night, the top of the mountain cools off faster than the forested land below. The cooler, denser air sinks, creating a wind down the mountainside.

4. In winter, the air inside your house is generally a lot drier (less humidity) than it is in summer. Here's the reason. If the outside temperature is low (winter), then the outside air can't hold much water vapor. So, even a relative humidity near 100% means there still isn't that much water vapor in the air.

If this air moves inside and then you heat the air (furnaces tend to do that), then you are increasing the amount of water vapor the air can hold without actually increasing the amount of water vapor in the air. Thus, the relative humidity goes way down, and the air is dry. The colder the outside air, the less water vapor it can hold, and the less the relative humidity once that air warms up inside.

5. If you listen to the weather report on the news, then you have probably heard the term **dew point**. The dew point is the temperature at which water condenses on a surface or, in practical terms, the temperature at which dew begins to form. Let's see how that works. During the day, the air is generally at a higher temperature than at night. This warmer air is able to hold more water vapor than cold air. When the sun goes down, the air cools off. As it cools, it can eventually reach a temperature at which the air is saturated (that might or might not happen). At that point, dew (water droplets) begins to form on the ground. So, the dew point really is a statement about the amount of water vapor in the air. A high dew point means there's lots of water vapor in the air. A low dew point means there's little water vapor in the air.

6. Maybe you've heard of **cloud seeding** in order to increase the possibility of rain. Just as condensation nuclei help water vapor form clouds, condensation nuclei also help the water vapor form into even larger water drops that fall as rain. To "seed" clouds, you simply shoot small particles up into the clouds, creating more condensation nuclei and increasing the chance of rain.

7. Perhaps you're saying to yourself, "Oh sure, it's fine to learn about clouds and dew point and such, but what about fog?" In case you're thinking that, here's an answer. **Fog** forms when air that is close to being saturated with water vapor cools beyond the dew point. This is common on a night when there's no cloud cover. This condition makes it easy for the ground to radiate heat into the atmosphere (more on that in the next chapter). The ground gets cold and cools the air above it. If that air gets cool enough, water droplets form and you get fog. If you live near San Francisco, you know that the fog generally "rolls in" toward the evening.[7] That's because, as the sun goes down, the land cools to a temperature below that of the ocean. As the ocean air, full of water vapor, encounters the cooler air from the land, the water vapor condenses and you get fog.

---

[7] Although conditions near the ocean are generally favorable for fog formation toward evening, fog can roll in at any time of day. That's because the relative temperature of the ocean and land depends on more than the differences between daytime and nighttime.

8. Okay, one last application. It's one you will only appreciate if you live where a snowstorm is followed the next day by intense sun. We get that in Colorado. In such an instance, when the sun is melting snow away from the roads, you get wispy clouds forming right over the surface of the road. This happens because the sun heats the roads much faster than it heats the air just above the roads. The water on the roads evaporates, and then condenses into "mini-clouds" immediately upon reaching the cold air just above the roads.

Large-Scale Weather[1]

I n the previous chapter, we dealt with how the properties of air and water affected small-scale weather such as the formation of clouds, the formation of fog, and how comfortable you feel at different times of the year. In this chapter, we're going to go global, talking about major interactions between the Sun and Earth, the resulting effects on large **air masses**, and how these major interactions help us figure out what the weather's going to be tomorrow. As I mentioned earlier in the book, when we apply science concepts to the real world, things don't always work out exactly as expected. On the other hand, we'll still get a pretty good overall picture of what's happening in large-scale weather.

"Rain. LOTS of rain. Everywhere. I suggest going out in pairs...
That's the 40-day outlook. Back to you, Nancy..."

---

[1] I owe much of my knowledge of large-scale weather patterns to a book by Jack Williams, titled *The Weather Book*. It's a USA Today book published by Vintage Books with a copyright of 1992. It's a great resource and will help you get a deeper understanding of just about all the concepts I deal with here.

Things to do before you read the science stuff

Figure 6.1

Figure 6.1

Get a Styrofoam ball that's at least 2 inches in diameter (the local hobby or craft store has lots of these), a pencil, and a table lamp. Push the pencil through the center of the ball (it might help if you sharpen the pencil first). Time to begin thinking of this Styrofoam ball as the Earth. Label the end of the ball with the point of the pencil poking through as the North Pole. Draw a dotted line around the middle of the ball to represent the equator. If you feel like it, go ahead and draw a few continents. "Why yes, Johnny, that's a really nice cow. It's not a cow, but the United States? Well then, it's a great drawing of the United States." See Figure 6.1.

Figure 6.2

Remove the shade from the lamp, set the lamp in the center of a darkened room, and turn on the lamp. Now hold the Styrofoam ball on the pencil at an angle, as shown in Figure 6.2.

Hold the ball at that angle and move around the lightbulb, noticing what parts of your "Earth" are illuminated as you complete your circle. Just in case you're not sure what I'm asking you to do, Figure 6.3 should make it clear.

Figure 6.3

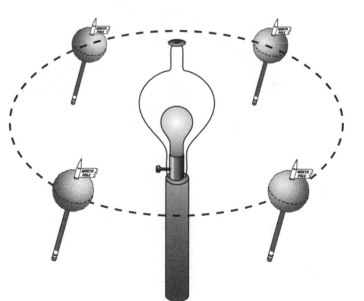

Next get a flashlight and a round balloon. Mark a north and south pole on the balloon, which will represent the Earth. The flashlight represents the Sun. Shine the sunlight on the "equator" of your balloon and then move the light so it shines near one of the poles (Figure 6.4). Notice how concentrated the light beam is at these two different positions.

Figure 6.4

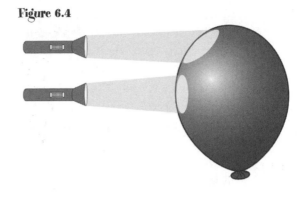

The science stuff

Now let's suppose that the lamp you're using represents the Sun, and the Styrofoam ball represents Earth (okay, I already told you the Styrofoam ball is the Earth). When Earth travels one time all the way around the Sun, that represents one year. You can see that, given the tilt of the Earth (yes, Earth really is tilted like this), different parts of Earth get different amounts of sunlight depending on the location of the Earth at different times of the year. Figure 6.5 labels the different positions that correspond to the different seasons in the northern and southern hemispheres.

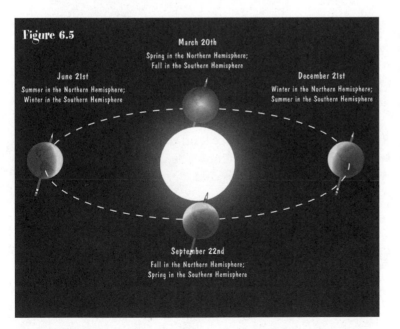

Figure 6.5

March 20th
Spring in the Northern Hemisphere;
Fall in the Southern Hemisphere

June 21st
Summer in the Northern Hemisphere;
Winter in the Southern Hemisphere

December 21st
Winter in the Northern Hemisphere;
Summer in the Southern Hemisphere

September 22nd
Fall in the Northern Hemisphere;
Spring in the Southern Hemisphere

What this demonstrates is that we go through the seasons (summer, fall, winter, and spring) because of the tilt of the Earth, not because Earth's distance from the Sun changes.[2]

SCI LINKS.
THE WORLD'S A CLICK AWAY

Topic: seasons

Go to: *www.scilinks.org*

Code: SFAWW18

---

[2] For the record, the distance between Earth and the Sun *does* change throughout the year, but that has nothing to do with the change of seasons.

In shining the flashlight on the balloon, you should have noticed that the light beam spreads out over a larger area when it hits the north and south poles of the Earth than when it hits the equator. Given that we get not just light, but heat,[3] from the Sun, this means that the poles always get less heat per area than the equator. We might expect, then, that the equator absorbs lots of heat and the poles absorb very little (Figure 6.6).

That does, in fact, happen. This leads to an important conclusion that helps us understand much of Earth's weather. The equator is a source of large-scale, warm air masses and the poles are a source of large-scale, cold air masses. Whether these air masses form over land or ocean determines how much humidity the air masses carry. It shouldn't be a surprise that air masses that form over water have lots of water vapor in them, and air masses that form over land are quite dry. Meteorologists classify these major air masses as follows:

Figure 6.6

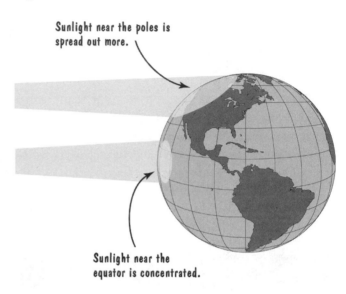

Sunlight near the poles is spread out more.

Sunlight near the equator is concentrated.

- Continental polar air masses—these form over land (hence the term continental) in the polar regions. Because they form at the poles, they're very cold, and because they form over land, they tend to have low humidity. When continental polar air masses in the north move southward in the winter, they lead to bitter cold temperatures in the northern United States.

- Maritime polar air masses—these form over oceans (hence the term maritime) in the polar regions. Because they form over the oceans, they tend to have high humidity. Also because they form over oceans, which tend to be much warmer than land in the

SCiLINKS.
THE WORLD'S A CLICK AWAY

Topic: air masses

Go to: *www.scilinks.org*

Code: SFAWW19

---

[3] I should mention that heat is basically the same kind of electromagnetic radiation that visible light is, and the two only differ in the frequency of radiation. Take a look at the *Stop Faking It!* book on Light for a more thorough explanation.

winter, they aren't nearly as cold as the continental polar air masses. People in the Pacific Northwest know all about the weather that results when these humid air masses reach land.

- Continental tropical air masses—as you can guess by their name, these air masses form over land near the equator. Because they form over land, they tend to have low humidity. The hot, dry air that reaches Mexico and the southwestern deserts in the United States comes from these air masses.

- Maritime tropical air masses—you guessed it; these air masses form over the oceans near the equator. They contain warm, humid air. These air masses account for the climate in states that border the Gulf of Mexico.

The interaction of these large air masses produces what's known as the **jet stream**. Before you can understand how that happens, though, you need to learn about a special force that is present on rotating things like the Earth. What say we move on and learn about that force?

More things to do before you read more science stuff

Grab a clean sheet of paper and a pen. You probably will also need a helper. Place the sheet of paper flat on a smooth surface and ask your helper to rotate the paper counterclockwise. While this is going on, take your pen and try to draw a straight line from the outside of the paper toward the center. Then try to draw a straight line from the center out to the edge, as shown in Figure 6.7. Tell your helper to stop rotating and take a look at your "straight" lines. Not so straight, huh?

Figure 6.7

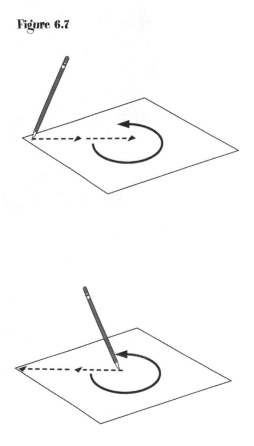

Just for kicks, turn the paper over, have your helper rotate the paper clockwise, and try those lines from the outside to the center and from the center to the outside. You should get a different result.

More science stuff

What you just discovered is that when you try and draw a straight line on a rotating surface, you end up with a curved line. One way of explaining this result is that anything moving on a rotating surface (your pen is moving and the paper is rotating) feels a force pushing it sideways. This force is known as the **Coriolis force**.[4] This force is sometimes called a "fictitious force," but it is very real to anyone or anything moving across a rotating surface. To feel this force, head to a merry-go-round and try walking from the edge to the center or from the center to the edge.

SCI LINKS.
THE WORLD'S A CLICK AWAY

Topic: Coriolis force

Go to: *www.scilinks.org*

Code: SFAWW20

The Earth just happens to be a rotating object. If you look down on the Earth from above the North Pole, Earth rotates counter-clockwise, as shown in Figure 6.8.[5]

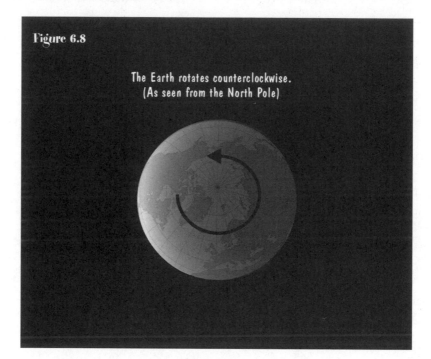

Figure 6.8

The Earth rotates counterclockwise.
(As seen from the North Pole)

---

[4] For an extended discussion of the Coriolis force, and other so-called fictitious forces, see the *Stop Faking It!* book on Force and Motion. Whether or not this force, or any force, truly exists depends on your "frame of reference." If you're in a frame of reference that is rotating, then the Coriolis force and something known as the centrifugal force are real forces. It might interest you to know that the force of gravity can exist or not exist depending on your frame of reference. In Einstein's theory of general relativity, the force of gravity does not exist if you use the "proper" frame of reference.

---

[5] If you're having trouble realizing that Earth rotates counterclockwise from this point of view, just think about the fact that sunrise occurs in the east and sunset occurs in the west. Sunrise and sunset are due to the rotation of the Earth, and only a counterclockwise rotation (as seen from above the North Pole) will make those happen in the proper order.

As you know from your experience with rotating paper and a pen, when you try to draw a straight line on something rotating counterclockwise, that line curves to the right. Using our new-found Coriolis force, we say that anything moving in the Northern Hemisphere on Earth feels a force to the right. See Figure 6.9.

Now let's look at the Southern Hemisphere of the Earth. If you look at Earth from above the South Pole, Earth is rotating clockwise. If you did as I asked and tried to draw a line on your paper when it was rotating clockwise, you found that the line curved to the left. Therefore, the Coriolis force in the southern hemisphere pushes moving things to the left, as in Figure 6.10.

Figure 6.9

In the Northern Hemisphere, the Coriolis force pushes moving objects to the right.

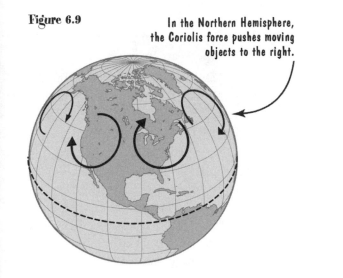

Figure 6.10

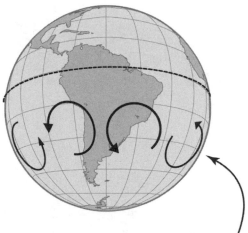

In the Southern Hemisphere, the Coriolis force pushes moving objects to the left.

SC*L*INKS.
THE WORLD'S A CLICK AWAY

Topic: atmospheric pressure and winds

Go to: *www.scilinks.org*

Code: SFAWW21

Topic: winds

Go to: *www.scilinks.org*

Code: SFAWW22

The Coriolis force has lots of applications where weather is concerned, but for now we'll see how it explains the jet stream. Do you recall (of course you do) that the Sun heats up the equator a whole lot more than it does the poles? That leads to cold air near the poles and warmer air as you near the equator.

Let's see what that implies for the air about 30,000 feet above the Earth's surface. In warm air masses, the

Figure 6.11

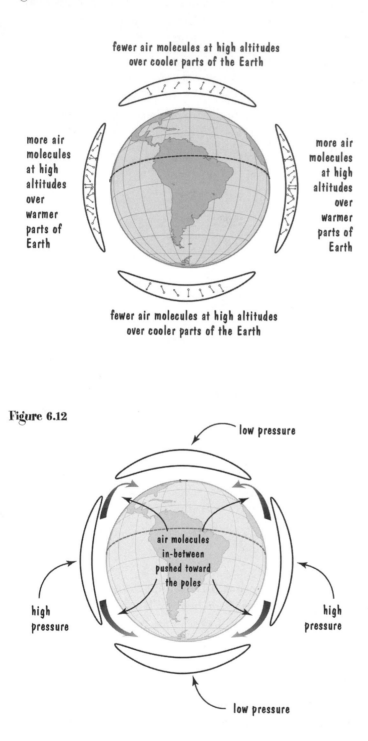

fewer air molecules at high altitudes
over cooler parts of the Earth

more air
molecules
at high
altitudes
over
warmer
parts of
Earth

more air
molecules
at high
altitudes
over
warmer
parts of
Earth

fewer air molecules at high altitudes
over cooler parts of the Earth

Figure 6.12

low pressure

air molecules
in-between
pushed toward
the poles

high
pressure

high
pressure

low pressure

fast-moving warm air at the surface pushes hard on its surroundings. In cold air masses, the slow-moving cold air doesn't push so hard on its surroundings. Air molecules at the surface push higher air molecules up to even higher altitudes. The harder the lower air molecules push, the more molecules there are at high altitudes. This means that at high altitudes, there are more air molecules above warm air masses than there are above cold air masses. Figure 6.11 illustrates this.

Remember that we're talking about the situation *way* above the surface of the Earth. There we have more air molecules in a given volume above warm air masses than we have air molecules at a given volume above cold air masses. More molecules means a higher pressure. Therefore, the high-altitude air molecules in between should be pushed from the warm air masses toward the cold air masses, or in our example, in a general direction from the equator toward the poles. Figure 6.12 shows this.

Once again, I'm referring to air pressure differences *across latitudes* at *high altitudes*, not any air pressure differences between air at different altitudes. So, the push we're talking about is a push horizontally, parallel to the surface of the Earth. Anyway, the air molecules in between the high- and low-pressure areas do what they're supposed to do. The only problem is, there's a Coriolis force that pushes these molecules to the right in the Northern Hemisphere and to the left in the Southern Hemisphere. That situation is shown in Figure 6.13.

If the Coriolis force were the only force acting, these in-between air molecules would just keep moving in a circle. We still have that pressure differ-ence, though, that's pushing the air from the equator toward the poles. What happens is that the force due to this pressure difference (known as the **pres-sure gradient force**) and the Coriolis force balance out, and the air molecules at high altitudes move from west to east across the Earth's surface (Fig-ure 6.14). The speed of this high-altitude wind is pretty fast—any-where from 80 to 200 miles per hour.

Figure 6.13

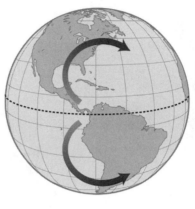

Coriolis force pushes the wind to the right in the Northern Hemisphere and to the left in the Southern Hemisphere.

Figure 6.14 is a bit mislead-ing, because it shows only one jet stream. In fact, there usu-ally are two jet streams in each hemisphere. There is a **polar jet stream** and a **subtropi-cal jet stream**. The polar jet stream tends to have much higher winds because the tem-perature gradient (taking into account differences in tempera-ture and the distance in which that difference occurs) of air masses that fuels it is greater than the temperature gradient

Figure 6.14

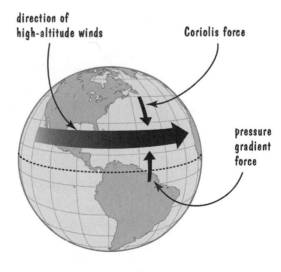

direction of high-altitude winds

Coriolis force

pressure gradient force

Figure 6.15

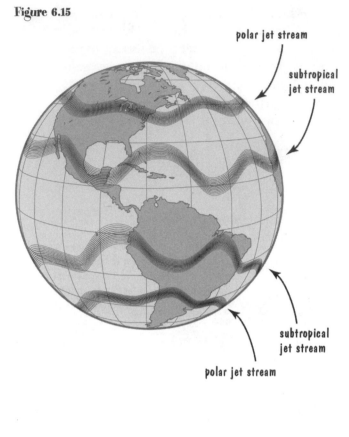

polar jet stream

subtropical
jet stream

subtropical
jet stream

polar jet stream

Figure 6.16

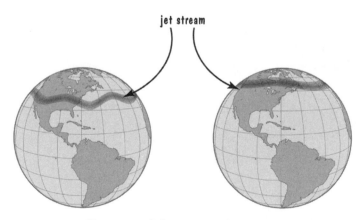

jet stream

The position of the jet stream determines
whether you'll experience cold or warm weather.

that fuels the subtropical jet stream. Figure 6.15 shows all of the jet streams on Earth.

One consequence of the existence of jet streams is that high- and low-pressure areas, and the storms that accompany these areas, move from west to east across the United States. To see what kind of weather might be headed your way, take a look at the weather map in your local newspaper. The weather that is occurring to the west of you is likely headed your way. Of course, storms don't move in exactly a straight line from west to east, so this isn't a foolproof method for determining your weather a few days from now.

Most weather maps and weather forecasters show the location of the polar jet stream. You'll notice that the jet stream is generally a wavy line. This wavy line marks the boundary between cold air from the north and warm air from the equator. If the polar jet stream "dips down" southward of your location in the winter, you are probably experiencing a cold snap. When the polar jet stream retreats northward, you're in for a warming trend. See Figure 6.16.

If you compare weather maps from summer and winter, you'll notice a difference in the position of the jet stream. In summer, the jet stream is farther north. Makes sense, because in summer, more of the Northern Hemisphere receives direct sunlight, and the battle between warm air from the equator and cold air from the North Pole shifts northward. Similarly, the jet stream is closer to the equator in winter months. Check out Figure 6.17.

Figure 6.17

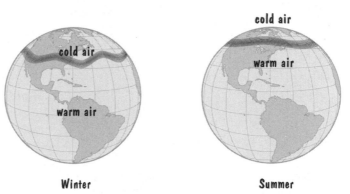

Winter

Summer

The jet stream is closer to the equator in the winter months.

Even more things to do before you read even more science stuff

As long as we're talking about weather maps, head to your newspaper and look at the national weather map. You should notice Hs and Ls. You'll also notice strange symbols that indicate warm fronts, cold fronts, and stationary fronts, which I'll discuss later in the chapter. For now, see if there's any pattern regarding the location of the Hs and Ls and the location of rain showers and snow showers. If you don't see a pattern, I'll give you a hint. You probably won't find rain or snow in the area right around an H, but you might find those things right around an L. Read on to see why.

SCI**LINKS.**
THE WORLD'S A CLICK AWAY

Topic: air masses and fronts

Go to: *www.scilinks.org*

Code: SFAWW23

Even more science stuff

The Hs on a weather map represent areas of high air pressure and the Ls represent areas of low air pressure (clever labeling, no?). For starters, let's figure out what might create these areas of high and low pressure. In general, you get a high-pressure area when the air is sinking. As the air sinks, it pushes on the air below it, increasing the pressure. Depending on the temperature of the ground in a high-pressure area, the H can be cold air or hot air. One thing that's consistent, though, is that you get very few clouds in high-pressure areas. Just think back to the miniature cloud you created in a 2-liter bottle in the previous chapter. When you push on the sides and increase the pressure, the cloud disappears.

Figure 6.18

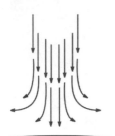

high-pressure area

Air sinks and the pressure
gets higher, making
condensation unlikely.

low-pressure area

Rising air cools and the
water vapor condenses.

The air in a low-pressure area is usually rising. Remember that as air rises, it pushes against the cooler air around it and creates more space for itself and gets cooler. That results in low pressure. If this air contains much water vapor, that water vapor condenses into clouds and possible rain or snow as it rises and cools off. Therefore, you are likely to find clouds and rain or snow showers around the Ls on the map. Figure 6.18 summarizes what happens in high- and low-pressure areas.

Now, because high pressure pushes things toward low pressure, you might expect that you would get winds blowing from Hs to Ls. That would be the case without the existence of the Coriolis force, as shown in Figure 6.19.

Because the Earth is rotating and there *is* a Coriolis force, however, we have a slightly different situation. Winds do begin blowing from high pressure to low pressure. In the Northern Hemisphere, those winds feel a Coriolis force to the right. Therefore, the air begins to move to the right as it enters the low-pressure area. Once it's moving to the right, we have a situation similar to that with the jet stream. You have a balance between the Coriolis force and the force due to the pressure difference between the H and L (again, this force is called a pressure gradient force). In this case, however, that

Figure 6.19

High
Pressure   winds   Low
                          Pressure

What the winds would do without the Coriolis force.

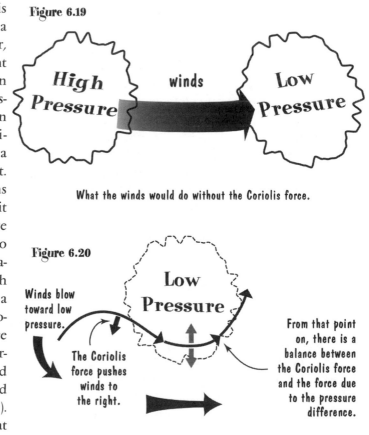

Figure 6.20

Winds blow
toward low
pressure.

Low
Pressure

The Coriolis
force pushes
winds to
the right.

From that point
on, there is a
balance between
the Coriolis force
and the force due
to the pressure
difference.

balance causes the air to move in a circle around the L, as shown in Figure 6.20. Hence, winds tend to circulate to the left around low-pressure areas.

Around high-pressure areas, we have a different situation. The winds blow *away* from high-pressure areas, and the Coriolis force pushes them to the right. If the Coriolis force kept doing its thing, the air would continue to be pushed to the right and would head back into the high-pressure area. The high pressure, however, is pushing the air outward. Again we have a balance, and the winds around a high-pressure area circle to the right, as shown in Figure 6.21.

Figure 6.21

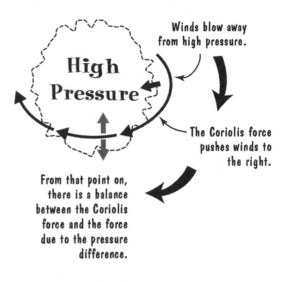

Winds blow away from high pressure.

The Coriolis force pushes winds to the right.

From that point on, there is a balance between the Coriolis force and the force due to the pressure difference.

The circulation around highs and lows just described applies to the situation at high altitudes. At lower altitudes, friction between the air and the Earth's surface slows the winds somewhat. This lessens the Coriolis force so it's smaller than the pressure gradient force. As a result, winds spiral in toward low-pressure areas and spiral out away from high-pressure areas near the surface of the Earth. See Figure 6.22.

A bit more on the circulation of winds around highs and lows in the next section. For now, you should at least realize that if the winds are blowing, you

Figure 6.22

Winds spiral inward around a low-pressure area near the Earth's surface.

Winds spiral outward around a high-pressuree area near the Earth's surface.

are likely in a transition area between a high-pressure area and a low-pressure area. As one replaces the other, the winds *do* change direction because of the different circulations around highs and lows. What this means, of course, is that the movie *Mary Poppins* was indeed based in scientific fact. That alone should make reading this book worthwhile. So, let's go fly a kite, up to the highest height ....

And even more things to do before you do even more science stuff

Get a clear baking pan and a sheet of cardboard. Cut the cardboard so it fits snugly in the baking pan, acting as a separator between two sides of the pan, as in Figure 6.23.

Next fill one pan, bowl, or pitcher with hot water and another with cold water. Put one color of food coloring in the hot water and a different color in the cold water. You'll need help with the next step. One person should hold the cardboard divider in place and the other should pour the hot and cold, different-colored water into opposite sides of the baking pan. While looking from the side, remove the cardboard divider (do this quickly before the water seeps around the cardboard divider). See Figure 6.24, and notice what happens to the hot and cold water after you remove the divider.

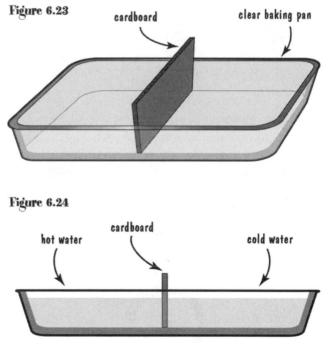

Figure 6.23

cardboard

clear baking pan

Figure 6.24

hot water

cardboard

cold water

And even more science stuff

Assuming you saw what I saw when I did the last activity, you found that, when mixed, hot water tends to rise over cold water. This should make sense in terms of our earlier activities, in which less dense liquids floated on top of more dense liquids. The hot water has fast-moving molecules that aren't confined. As a result, they have a lower density than the cold, slower-moving molecules. Less dense liquids get pushed upward by more dense liquids. The cold water pushes the hot water upward, and the hot water ends up on top. Look at Figure 6.25.

Figure 6.25

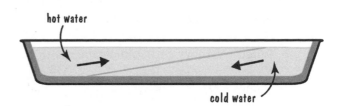

hot water

cold water

And even more science stuff

You know already that weather maps contain Hs and Ls, and that these high- and low-pressure areas move across the Earth. As they do this, the high- and low-pressure areas take with them the winds that circulate around the pressure areas. These high- and low-pressure areas are large scale, meaning that they can each cover a major portion of the United States. Within and between those high- and low-pressure areas are regions that consist of cold air, warm air, dry air, humid air, and all combinations of those descriptions. There are so many factors that go into the creation of these areas of air, that it won't do us much good to address the issue here. Suffice to say that these smaller-scale air masses originate from the large-scale cold and warm regions of air that come from the poles and the equator, and get caught up in the winds the surround the major high- and low-pressure areas.

The small-scale areas of warm, cold, humid, and dry air that are associated with different major high- and low-pressure areas often come in contact. These points of contact are called **fronts**. A **cold front** is a place where cold air is overtaking warm air. A **warm front** is where warm air is overtaking cold air. A **stationary front** is where cold air and warm air are meeting, but neither one is displacing the other. Figure 6.26 shows the symbols for these different fronts you'll see on a weather map.[6]

Figure 6.26

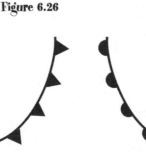

cold front   warm front   stationary front

---

[6] There is a fourth type of front, known as an occluded front, in which warm, cool, and cold air masses come together. Occluded fronts are less common than other fronts.

In the activity you just did, you saw what happens when cold air and warm air meet. Actually, you saw what happens when cold water and hot water meet, but remember that air and water behave a whole lot like each other. Anyway, the hot water rises above the cold water because it's less dense than the cold water. When warm air and cold air meet, the same thing happens. The warm air rises above the cold air, as in Figure 6.27.

Figure 6.27

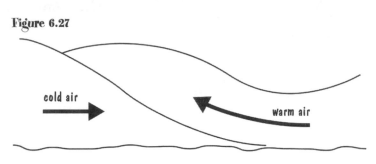

What happens next depends on the temperature difference between the cold air and warm air, and especially on the humidity of the cold and warm air. If the warm air is humid (often the case, since much of the warm air we get in the United States originates over the Gulf of Mexico), then the rising and resultant cooling of that humid air results in clouds and possibly rain or snow. So, whether you have a warm front, a cold front, or a stationary front, you have a situation that's favorable for precipitation. Figure 6.28 shows the various possibilities at these fronts.

Figure 6.28

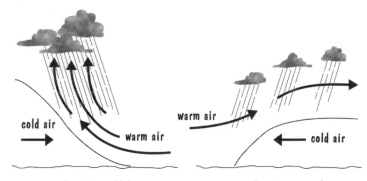

an advancing cold front   an advancing warm front

At a cold front, where cold air is overtaking warm air, the warm air rises rapidly and cools rapidly. This can create big thunderstorms in the summer and snowfalls in the

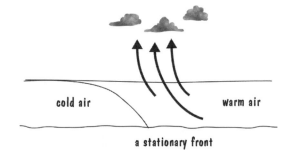

a stationary front

winter. At a warm front, where warm air is overtaking cold air, the warm air rises more gradually. This generally leads to steady, long-lasting rains rather than thunderstorms in the summer and steady snowfalls in the winter.

Chapter Summary

- Sunlight hits Earth unevenly. The equator receives more concentrated sunlight than do the poles.

- The different temperatures of different parts of the Earth during different seasons depend on the position of Earth with respect to the Sun and the tilt of Earth's axis. The seasons have nothing to do with how far Earth is from the Sun at different times of the year.

- Because of the interaction between the Sun and Earth's atmosphere, large air masses form on the Earth. These can be high- or low-pressure air masses and can contain dry or humid air, depending on where they form. These large air masses, their movement, and their interactions are responsible for much of Earth's weather.

- When considering motion on an object moving in a circle (such as air moving across the surface of the Earth), a special force known as the Coriolis force comes into play. In the Northern Hemisphere, the Coriolis force pushes moving objects to the right. In the Southern Hemisphere, the Coriolis force pushes moving objects to the left.

- The jet streams are concentrated channels of high-altitude, high-speed winds that move primarily from west to east. The jet stream is a result of high-altitude pressure differences between air at different latitudes, coupled with the Coriolis force. Because of the jet streams, major weather systems move from west to east across the Earth.

- The surface of the Earth is dotted with high- and low-pressure areas. High-pressure areas are generally associated with clear skies and low-pressure areas are generally associated with cloudy skies and precipitation. Winds tend to blow clockwise and spiral outward around high-pressure areas and winds tend to blow counterclockwise and spiral in around low-pressure areas.

- Places where cold and warm air masses meet are called *fronts* and are usually accompanied by precipitation. At fronts, warm air tends to rise up above cold air.

Applications

1. The fact that the sunlight is more concentrated at the equator year-round and less concentrated at the poles year-round creates more-or-less permanent high- and low-pressure areas. The poles are consistently high-pressure areas because there the cold air sinks down and gets even colder as it nears the cold ground. All that sinking of cold air creates a high-pressure area. As this cold air spreads southward, it eventually gets warmer as it encounters warmer ground. When the air warms, it rises (pushed up by cold air). As it rises, it creates more room for itself and cools (we covered that process in the chapter) and is therefore a low-pressure area. What you have is a large-scale convection cell. Such convection cells result in all that rain they get in Seattle. Figure 6.29 shows this.

    Because the sunlight at the equator is more concentrated, the air above that warmer ground rises (pushed up again) and is a low-pressure area. As that air rises, the water vapor in it will condense if it cools below the dew point, resulting in the formation of clouds and the potential for lots of rain. These low-pressure areas are also the start of another convection cell, one that rises above the equator and drops over the southwestern deserts in the United States and over the Sahara desert in Africa. The winds that accompany these equatorial convection cells are known as the **trade winds**. Figure 6.30 might help.

Figure 6.29

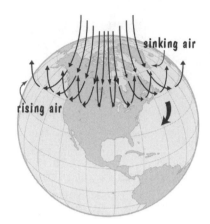

Figure 6.30

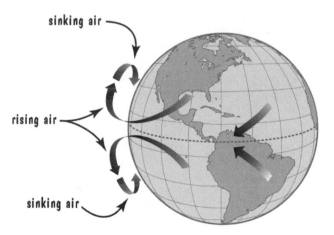

2. The jet stream isn't called that just because it seemed to be a catchy name. Jets generally fly at around 30,000 feet above the Earth's surface. If you're flying a jet from west to east, you can get a big ol' tailwind from the jet stream. You can cut back on the engines, save lots of fuel, and still move at a high speed. On the other hand, if you're moving from east to west, you have to work against those high winds. In fact, it might be smarter to move north or south, avoiding the jet stream, so you don't have to deal with that really big head wind. And while we're on the subject, one source of airplane turbulence (that stuff that makes me turn on the air vent and stop reading) is a jet crossing over the jet stream, where the wind speeds can change dramatically in a short distance.

3. The jet stream drags storms from west to east. Along the way, those storms encounter mountain ranges. Let's look at what happens when a storm encounters a mountain range. Obviously, the air has to travel up the mountainside. As the air rises, it cools. As the air cools, water vapor in the air condenses, and often results in precipitation such as rain and snow. As the air passes over the mountain range, it loses more and more of its moisture. By the time a storm passes over a mountain range, it often has little moisture left to deposit in the form of rain or snow. As this dry air descends on the other side of a mountain range, it warms quickly. So, there's a reason that the desert regions of the United States, such as eastern Washington State and the inland deserts of California and Arizona, occur east of major mountain ranges.

Figure 6.31

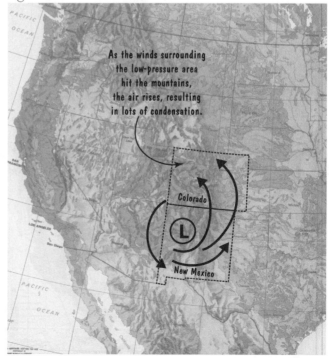

As the winds surrounding the low-pressure area hit the mountains, the air rises, resulting in lots of condensation.

4. Not that it means much to anyone outside of my home state of Colorado, but there is one weather pattern in the winter that assures us on the eastern side of the continental divide lots of snow. It's called an "Albuquerque low." That means there's a low-pressure area centered on Albuquerque, New Mexico. Low-pressure areas bring snow in winter. They also bring winds that circle counterclockwise around the low-

pressure area. These winds cover a wide circle, one that includes Colorado. When these counterclockwise winds encounter the Rocky Mountains, the air rises. The resultant cooling causes the water vapor in that air to condense and give up its moisture in the form of snow.[7] Figure 6.31 explains it all.

---

[7] For the record, I have no complaints about snow. After a summer of fearing my house would burn down from nearby forest fires, I welcome all forms of precipitation.

The Severe Stuff

S o far, I've dealt with small-scale and large-scale patterns of weather. What seems to interest people most, though, are the "special" events related to weather. Those special events include thunderstorms, tornadoes, hurricanes, floods, and droughts. I'm not going to address floods and droughts, but you should have a handle on the first three items by the time you finish this chapter.

There aren't many activities for you to do in this chapter. The reason is that you already have many of the experiences you need to understand the concepts in this chapter. Think of this chapter as "Applications plus." I should also mention again that I won't necessarily be covering some of the "usual stuff" contained in books on weather, such as scales for measuring wind speeds, scales for measuring hurricane damage, and the formation of lightning. The reason? This isn't your usual book on weather. What I've tried to do is tie together basic

Neither thunderstorm...

or tornado...

nor hurricane...

shall keep junk mail from being delivered!

physical concepts regarding air and water and apply them to weather concepts in a way that might give you a perspective not contained in other books. Many existing books on weather will provide you with that other information.

Things to do before you read the science stuff

Get two empty 2-liter bottles and a connector known as a "tornado tube." You can find these things at hobby or science stores, and they're pretty cheap. A tornado tube is just a round tube of plastic with threads on each end and a constriction in the middle. Figure 7.1 shows a drawing of a tornado tube and a drawing of what you can use as a substitute, consisting of a narrow section of pipe insulation with a metal washer in the center.

Remove the labels from your 2-liter bottles and fill one of them with water. Screw the tornado tube onto the one filled with water (slide the pipe insulation over the opening if you're using that option) and then screw the empty bottle on top, as shown in Figure 7.2.

Now even though you might have used this contraption before, follow along with me before you go creating a tornado. Quickly turn the bottles over so the bottle with water is on top. Set it on a table and just watch for a while. Does water flow all at once from the top bottle to the bottom one? No? What's it doing, then? Does *any* water go from top to bottom? (Probably.) What do you notice about the top bottle whenever a small amount of water goes from the top to the bottom?

Okay, now take this thing and swirl it around as shown in Figure 7.3. Once a tornado-shaped funnel forms in the water in

Figure 7.1

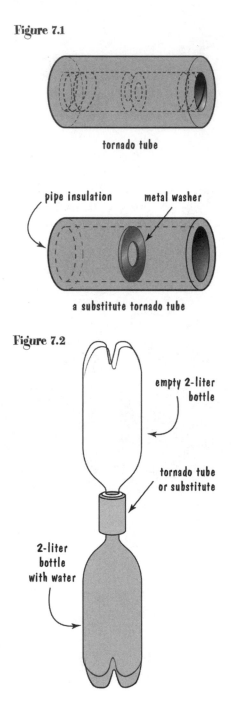

tornado tube

pipe insulation   metal washer

a substitute tornado tube

Figure 7.2

empty 2-liter bottle

tornado tube or substitute

2-liter bottle with water

the top bottle, set the thing down and watch. **Figure 7.3**
Do this a few times as you watch the water go
from top to bottom. Does the water go through
the center of the connector or down the sides?
If water isn't going through the center, is *any-thing* going through there? Just for kicks, add a
few Monopoly houses and perhaps a witch on
a bicycle to your bottle and see what they do
once the tornado starts.

The science stuff

When you turned your 2-liter bottles connected
with a tornado tube[1] over, the water from the
top bottle didn't immediately fall down into the
bottom bottle. The reason? There was *air* in the
bottom bottle. That air exerts a pressure and
doesn't just "give in" when something is pushing down on it. Now occasionally a few drops of
water will fall into the bottom bottle. If you were
a good little observer, you noticed that each time
water went from the top to the bottom, air
bubbles floated up through the top bottle. Makes
sense, because air has to escape to the upper
bottle in order for water to move down.

Come on, Baby! Let's do the Twirl!

Topic: storms

Go to: *www.scilinks.org*

Code: SFAWW24

    Would you call this a "stable" situation? Are
your two bottles likely to remain with the water
in the top bottle and air in the bottom bottle
for a long time? If you left this contraption set up for a few hours, would you
expect the water to still be mostly in the top bottle? Heck, no. What you have is
a very *unstable* situation. You have a dense substance (the water) on top of a
much less dense substance (the air in the bottom bottle). Dense fluids tend to
push down and displace less-dense fluids, so it's only a matter of time before the
water ends up in the bottom bottle.

    This is exactly the kind of situation that leads to thunderstorms on the
Earth. Sometimes you get a situation where there's a layer of cold air (dense) on
top of a layer of warm, humid air (not so dense). Spring and summer are good

---

[1] Although we started with a device known as a tornado tube, I'm going to begin by using your
experience to explain thunderstorms prior to explaining tornadoes.

times for this kind of situation, because high altitude air is still cold from winter, and low altitude air just gets warmer as it picks up heat from the increasingly warmer ground. See Figure 7.4.

Figure 7.4

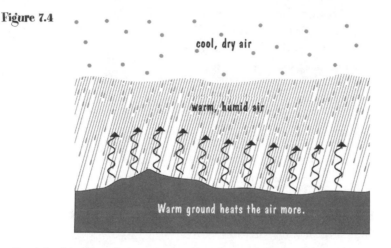

In this situation, it's only a matter of time before some of that warm, humid air breaks through the colder air on top. Once that happens, the warm air keeps rising, being pushed up by the cooler air surrounding it. As the warm, humid air rises, it cools (remember why that happens?). As it cools, the water vapor in the air can cool to the dew point and condense into water droplets. If you'll recall from Chapter 5, when water vapor condenses into water, it gives off heat (the latent heat of vaporization). That heat slows the cooling of the rising air, making it rise even faster and higher. As this air rises even higher, you get more condensation. See Figure 7.5.

Figure 7.5

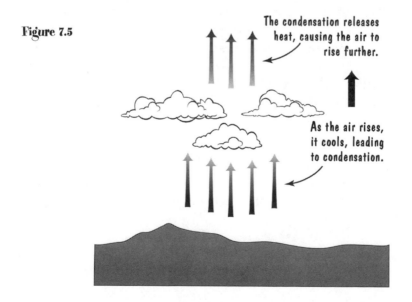

At the top of this rising column of cooling and condensing air, you get enough cold air and water that the whole thing begins to sink back toward Earth. That sinking completes a *convection cell,* something covered in Chapter 5. Another name for this particular convection cell is a thunderstorm. Check out Figure 7.6.

As the cold air on the outside of our thunderstorm sinks, some of the water in it encounters warmer air and evaporates. Knowing all you do about changes of state, you know that evaporation is a cooling process (the reverse of condensation). Therefore, the sinking air becomes even colder, and therefore denser, leading to big ol' downdrafts accompanying the thunderstorm.

Before we move on to tornadoes, let's cover a couple more things regarding thunderstorms. First, they seldom occur as an isolated convection cell as drawn in Figure 7.6. What usually happens is that the cold air descending on the edge of the thunderstorm then moves along the ground, encountering more warm, humid

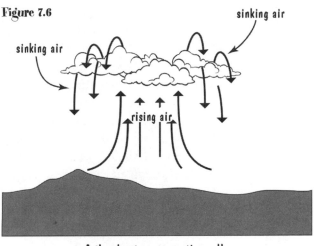

Figure 7.6

A thunderstorm convection cell

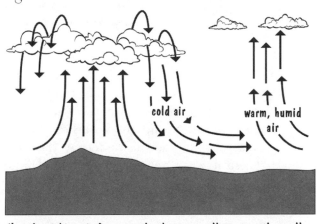

Figure 7.7

How the sinking air from one thunderstorm cell creates other cells.

air. That encounter pushes the warm, humid air upward, resulting in another convection cell (Figure 7.7). So, most thunderstorms are "multi-cell" thunderstorms, which explains why the rain and/or hail gets stronger, weaker, and stronger as the storm passes through.

The second thing to cover regarding thunderstorms is how hail forms. Sometimes, the updrafts in thunderstorms get so strong that the humid air in the center rises to incredible heights. The higher this air rises, the colder it gets (remember, it gets colder and colder the farther you are from the surface of the

Earth). That means the water vapor condenses into water, and then the water becomes ice. As the ice particles rise up, they gather more and more water droplets that turn into ice as they join up. At some point, these ice particles become heavy enough to fall back down. On the way down, they can encounter strong updrafts that push them back up. On the way up, more water vapor condenses and freezes on the ice particles and they become larger and sink again. These newly formed hail stones can cycle up and down a number of times before actually falling to the ground. The more cycles, the larger the hailstones. If you cut open a hailstone, you can often see the layers that result from the stone cycling through updrafts and downdrafts. By the way, if you have never had golf-ball-sized hail hit your house, you haven't lived. It sorta sounds like the neighbor kid has finally lost it and is chucking large rocks onto your roof.

Topic: tornadoes

Go to: *www.scilinks.org*

Code: SFAWW25

Tornadoes require the same kinds of conditions as severe thunderstorms—a layer of cold air on top of a layer of warm, humid air. In fact, thunderstorms and tornadoes many times go hand in hand. What gets a tornado started is a combination of winds that start a circular motion, accompanied by a break in the unstable conditions that allows warm, humid air to rise. It's just like the situation with the 2-liter bottles. When the water is on top, the conditions are right for a tornado to occur. Just the right circular motion to get the tornado started is all you need. As you noticed with the bottles, once that circular motion gets going (it's called a **vortex** by the way), there is a rapid transfer of lower density stuff (the air in the bottom bottle) upward and of higher density stuff (the water) downward. You should also have noticed that once your "tornado" is underway, the water flows down on the outside edges as the air moves up in the center. Gee, kind of like a convection cell, huh?

Contrary to what you might think, tornadoes do not get their spin from the Coriolis force. If they did, then all tornadoes would spin in the same direction (counterclockwise) in the Northern Hemisphere. They don't, though. Tornadoes have been observed that spin in either direction. This is not unlike the myth that all drains in the Northern Hemisphere spin in one direction. A little bit of experimentation will tell you this isn't true. Depending on how you start the rotation, you can get a drain to spin either clockwise or counterclockwise. It all has to do with the starting conditions. With tornadoes, the conditions under which they form are so unstable that it's possible for them to spin in either direction.

We all know that Dorothy and her house rose up inside a tornado. The reason for that is that a tornado represents a region of really low air pressure. That low air pressure is due to two effects. One is the warm air inside that's rising upward. The other is due to our old friend Bernoulli. That high-velocity wind spinning around the tornado results in very low air pressure compared to the surrounding air. By the way, the winds in a tornado can reach speeds of around 300 miles per hour. That's twice the speed of the winds in a major hurricane.

We all know that tornadoes destroy houses and trailers and just about every other building they encounter. Knowing what you do about the Bernoulli Effect, you might think that houses get blown apart because the high winds outside create a low pressure area (Bernoulli), resulting in the higher pressure inside the house blowing the roof upward and the walls outward. Continuing your analysis as you watch an approaching tornado, you might be tempted to open windows in the house in order to equalize the pressure. Not a good idea, though. It turns out that houses are rather leaky places when it comes to equalizing air pressure, and any difference in air pressure caused by the Bernoulli Effect is readily equalized via the various drafty places in your house. The damage caused by tornadoes is due mostly just to the high winds themselves. Those winds can tear a roof off a house simply because of their speed. So, instead of opening windows, head to the basement!

More things to do before you read more science stuff

This is a pretty simple things-to-do section. Just try to recall all you know about hurricanes. In case you're feeling lazy, here are a few things associated with hurricanes. They are really large and they form near the equator. They spin counterclockwise in the Northern Hemisphere, and they have an "eye" where the winds are calm. Hurricanes move from east to west and then follow a path that curves upward and to the right in the Northern Hemisphere. When a hurricane reaches land, it weakens.

More science stuff

The conditions that create hurricanes are similar to those that create tornadoes, but they're even more specialized. First, you need very warm, very humid air lying underneath a layer of cold air. The only place you'll find air humid enough and warm enough is near the equator, over the oceans. The water that's making this air humid has to be above 80 degrees Fahrenheit, and it has to be warm to a substantial depth given that a hurricane stirs up water well below the surface. Finally, the existing winds above a forming hurricane have to all be blowing pretty much at the same speed and in the same direction, all the way up to high altitudes. If this weren't the case, the winds at different altitudes would tend to tear apart the hurricane before it gets to any reasonable size. And of course hurricanes are a whole lot larger than tornadoes.

Topic: hurricanes

Go to: *www.scilinks.org*

Code: SFAWW26

Okay, so let's see how these things form. It starts with the warm, humid air rising up through a layer of cold air, just as with a regular thunderstorm. Also like a thunderstorm, the rising air *gains energy* (heats up) as the water vapor in it condenses. That causes the air to rise faster.[2]

At the base of the forming hurricane, you have cooler air pushing in toward the rising, warm, humid air. Because of the Coriolis force, that air gets pushed to the right (in the Northern Hemisphere) as it enters the low pressure area. Just as with air entering any low-pressure area in the Northern Hemisphere, there is a balance between the Coriolis force and the force due to the pressure difference. The result is that the air circles counterclockwise around the center. Again, the friction between the air and the water or land slows the winds and reduces the Coriolis force somewhat, resulting in the wind spiraling in toward the center rather than just staying a constant distance from the center. See Figure 7.8.

Okay, what about the eye of a hurricane? How come things calm down as the eye passes over you? Well, as high winds spiral inward and rise up around the outside of the hurricane, the eye is an area of strong downdrafts. These downdrafts result in an area of high pressure, and as we've seen before, high-pressure areas tend to produce little in the way of precipitation.

That's about all there is to the formation of a hurricane. As long as the storm stays over warm water and as long as the prevailing winds at higher altitudes don't tear it apart, it will continue to grow in size. The path a hurricane takes is due to two things. The first are "steering currents," which are prevailing winds that guide the storm as a whole. A major source of these steering currents are the *trade winds* (discussed in the Applications section of

Figure 7.8

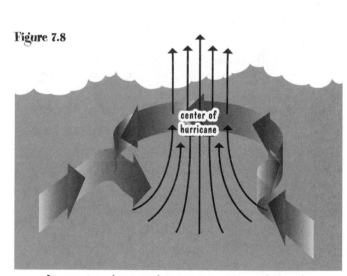

Air entering a hurricane low-pressure area is pushed to the right by the Coriolis force. After that, the balance between the Coriolis force and the force due to pressure differences makes the wind circulate counterclockwise.

---

[2] You might remember that I told you a while ago that the condensation of water vapor is what gives a hurricane its energy. Well, here's that happening.

Chapter 6), which blow hurricanes from east to west. The second is that the Coriolis force causes the path to curve upward and to the right. How far west hurricanes go before turning significantly northward depends largely on the size of a major high-pressure area that forms in the Atlantic Ocean, known as the **Bermuda High**. If this high-pressure area is large, hurricanes tend to swing farther west before turning north. If this high-pressure area is small, hurricanes make a smaller circle, as shown in Figure 7.9.[3]

The only thing left to explain is why hurricanes lose strength when they hit land. You might already have figured out the answer. When hurricanes hit land, they run out of their source of high humidity (the ocean). Because the condensation of water vapor is such a major source of energy for hurricanes, they weaken considerably when the major source of their water vapor disappears.

Okay, that's it for this book. We've gone from basic concepts regarding the behavior of air and water to different applications of those concepts to the Earth's weather. You should note that I've left out a number of weather concepts, one being the types of clouds and how they form. I feel comfortable leaving that out because it's covered in just about every single book on weather in existence. If you understand what I've gone over in *this* book, you'll have no trouble understanding the treatment of clouds in other books. The other major omission is *global warming*. There are a few reasons I'm not dealing with that here. The first is that, in order to give you sufficient background to understand not just what global warming is, but all the arguments surrounding it, I would have to double the size of this book. The second is that scientists do not even agree whether or not global warming is occurring. Again, it would take

Figure 7.9

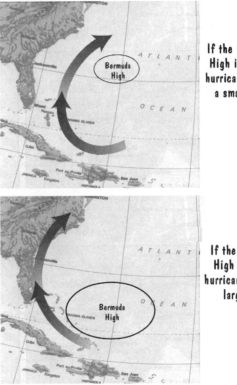

If the Bermuda High is small, hurricanes make a small arc.

If the Bermuda High is large, hurricanes make a large arc.

---

[3] Remember that winds tend to circulate counterclockwise around high-pressure areas, and actually spiral outward when the high-pressure area is near the surface of the Earth.

many pages just to discuss the different methods of measuring the temperature of the Earth, and why those different methods might or might not give reliable results. Third, even if global warming *is* occurring, scientists do not agree on the mechanism. It could be variations in the intensity of the Sun, it could be due to accumulation of so-called greenhouse gases, or it could be due to various other factors—that is, if it's really happening. Finally, the subject is so closely intertwined with politics that I would undoubtedly offend lots of people no matter what side I came down on. Who wants that?

Chapter Summary

- Thunderstorms and tornadoes form when you have the unstable condition of cool, dry air on top of warm, humid air.

- Thunderstorms and tornadoes consist of one or more large convection cells. The condensation of water vapor inside the cells releases heat that keeps the convection cells going.

- Hail forms when the updrafts in a thunderstorm are large enough that water droplets form into ice and then cycle through several updrafts and downdrafts.

- Hurricanes are large versions of thunderstorms that form over oceans near the equator. They move in a clockwise path in the Northern Hemisphere due to the trade winds and the Coriolis force. Hurricanes are fueled by water vapor condensation and therefore lose a great deal of energy when they hit land.

Applications

Don't look here. I already told you this chapter was pretty much nothing but applications to start with!

Glossary

adhesion. The attraction liquid molecules have for other substances, such as glass or paper.

air masses. Large areas of air that can be dry or humid, and contain high or low pressure areas.

air pressure. Pressure exerted by air molecules. How hard these molecules push, and how many molecules are in a given volume, determine the size of the air pressure.

atmosphere. The name given to all of the air surrounding the Earth. Also something people look for in restaurants.

atmospheric pressure. The pressure caused by the weight of the atmosphere above a certain position. At sea level, atmospheric pressure is about 100,000 newtons per square meter, or 14.7 pounds per square inch.

bends. A condition in which dissolved carbon dioxide in your bloodstream comes out of solution too fast. This results from rising too quickly to the surface when SCUBA diving.

Bermuda High. A high pressure area in the Atlantic Ocean that, by its size, helps determine the path of hurricanes.

Bernoulli Effect. The process in which a fluid moves quickly parallel to a given surface, resulting in a reduced air pressure perpendicular to the surface. The higher the speed, the lower the pressure.

buoyant force. An upward force that a fluid exerts on objects immersed in it. The buoyant force is equal to the weight of the displaced fluid.

Cartesian diver. A device in which an object in a bottle sinks when you squeeze on the bottle and rises when you release the bottle. Also, a SCUBA diver who works solely in Euclidian space (that's an inside joke that you'll only get if you have a strong background in physics or math. If I explained it, you would think it was stupid, but geeks have their own sense of humor.).

change of state. The transformation of a solid to a liquid, a liquid to a gas, a gas to a liquid, or a liquid to a solid. Also, what people often do when they change jobs, hear of the presence of new jobs, or just plain get tired of the weather where they live.

cloud seeding. The process of shooting small particles into clouds so that these particles can serve as condensation nuclei and promote rain or snow.

cold front. A situation where you have a mass of cold air advancing upon a mass of warm air.

condensation. The process of a gas changing into a liquid. With weather, this usually refers to water vapor changing into liquid water.

condensation nuclei. Small particles that serve as locations on which water vapor can attach and form into water droplets. Lots of things can serve as condensation nuclei, including salt molecules, smoke, and smog.

convection. The process in which a denser fluid pushes a less-dense fluid upward. As the less-dense fluid rises, it sometimes cools, becoming denser, and sinks.

convection cell. A complete, circular path of convection.

Coriolis force. A force that appears when you try to move across a spinning surface. The Coriolis force is responsible for the direction of the jet streams, the circulation of winds around high and low pressure areas, and the general path that hurricanes take.

density. Either the mass per unit volume or the weight per unit volume of a substance or object.

dew point. The temperature at which water vapor condenses into liquid water. The dew point is an indirect measure of relative humidity.

eardrum. A membrane, also known as the tympanic membrane, that divides the inner ear from the outer ear. The eardrum distorts in response to pressure variations both in and outside the ear.

equation of continuity. An equation that represents the change in speed as a fluid moves from one cross-sectional area to another. The equation is $A_1v_1 = A_2v_2$.

Eustachian tube. A tube that leads from your inner ear to your sinus cavities and mouth.

evaporation. The process of a liquid changing to a gas, accomplished by the addition of heat to the liquid.

fluid. A generic name that applies to substances that behave in certain ways, among them flowing smoothly in and around things. Physicists usually consider both liquids and gases to be fluids.

fog. The condensation of water vapor close to the ground or water. Also, the name of a book and movie my wife and daughter thought was scary, but which

I found somewhat dumb.

force. Any push, pull, shove, nudge, or yank. Something you don't want to use excessively if you are in a position of authority.

front. A place where warm and cold air masses meet. Also, the name of a Woody Allen movie about blacklisting after WWII.

g. The symbol used to represent the acceleration of an object falling only under the influence of gravity. *g* is equal to 9.8 meters per second squared or 32 feet per second squared.

gases. Substances in which the molecules move around so much that they don't interact except when they collide.

gravitational force. The attractive force the Earth exerts on objects.

heat. The name given to the energy transferred from a hotter object or substance to a cooler object or substance.

humidity. The amount of water vapor in the air.

hurricane. A bigger storm than a tornado, and one that lasts a lot longer. Hurricanes form over warm water and then head toward Florida. Also, a drink that you can get at Pat O'Brien's in New Orleans that will make you forget where you are.

hydrogen. An atom that's part of water molecules and that's part of a hydrogen gas molecule. In a water molecule, the hydrogen end of the molecule is positive.

hygrometer. A device used to measure humidity.

ideal gas. A gas that behaves according to the kinetic theory of gases. The kind of gas that other gases must aspire to be like.

jet stream. Concentrated, high-altitude streams of fast-moving wind that blow from west to east across both the Northern and Southern Hemispheres. The jet streams are primarily responsible for the fact that major weather features move from west to east across the Earth.

kinetic energy. A form of energy that depends on the square of the speed of whatever you're talking about.

kinetic theory of gases. A scientific model of how gas molecules behave. In the model, the gas molecules move independently and only interact when they collide with one another or with the walls of a container.

latent heat of fusion. The heat that is lost or gained when a substance changes from a liquid to a solid or from a solid to a liquid. Also, something steamy that is buried in your psyche, having to do with fusion.

Glossary

latent heat of vaporization. The heat that is lost or gained when a substance changes from a gas to a liquid or from a liquid to a gas.

liquids. Substances in which the molecules move around a whole lot more than in solids, and which tend to take the shape of any container they're in.

mass. A measure of the amount of "stuff" in an object. For a complete understanding of the concept of mass, you need to understand Newton's second law.

mass density. The mass of an object or substance divided by its volume.

nitrogen. A gas that makes up about 80% of the Earth's atmosphere.

oxidation. The process of burning, in which oxygen from the air and carbon from the substance burning combine to create carbon dioxide and water.

oxygen. An atom that's part of water molecules and that's part of an oxygen gas molecule. In a water molecule, the oxygen end of the molecule is negative. Oxygen makes up about 20 percent of the Earth's atmosphere. Pure oxygen is what athletes breathe when they come to Colorado and get really tired because of the altitude.

paper chromatography. The process in which a liquid "climbs" up a paper strip (due to adhesion), resulting in the separation of the components of the liquid due to the different weights of the components.

polar jet stream. One of two jet streams in each hemisphere that mark the division between warm and cold air in the hemispheres. The polar jet streams tend to have much higher winds than the subtropical jet streams.

polar molecules. Molecules that have a charge separation, resulting in one end of the molecule being positive and the other being negative. Also, any molecules that hang around the Arctic Circle. These molecules tend to have white fur.

pressure. The total force acting on a given area divided by that area. Something you experience when others are expecting a lot from you.

pressure gradient force. A force due to pressure differences between high and low pressure areas.

relative humidity. The amount of water vapor in the air compared to the amount of water vapor the air can hold at maximum capacity. The formula for relative humidity is $relative\ humidity = \frac{amount\ of\ water\ vapor\ actually\ in\ the\ air}{amount\ of\ water\ vapor\ in\ the\ air\ when\ it's\ saturated} \times 100\%$. Also, relatives who make you sweat.

siphon. A tube used to transfer liquid from one container to another, using the force of gravity.

solids. Substances that retain their shape, and in which the molecules pretty much stay put.

stationary front. A situation where you have a mass of cold air meeting a mass of warm air, and neither mass is making any headway.

subtropical jet stream. One of two jet streams in each hemisphere, that are closer to the equator and usually contains weaker winds than the polar jet streams.

surface tension. A phenomenon in which water or other liquid develops a "skin" due to the attraction of the liquid molecules for one another.

temperature. How hot or cold something is. To be more specific, temperature is a measure of how fast the molecules in a substance are moving. The faster they move, the higher the temperature. In a gas, the temperature is defined as the average kinetic energy of the molecules.

tornado. A big ol' storm that results when a cool air mass sits on top of a warm, humid air mass. When the warm air breaks through the unstable situation, you have a good chance of a tornado.

trade winds. Winds that blow from East to West near the Equator, largely a result of convection cells near the Equator. Also, the name of a motel in Tulsa, Oklahoma, at which I always hoped my dad would stop on our cross-country car trips because they had a neat pool.

volume. The amount of space a substance or an object takes up. A button on the remote that used to be a knob on the television.

vortex. The circular flow of a fluid around its center, as in a tornado or a whirlpool.

warm front. A situation where you have a mass of warm air advancing upon a mass of cold air.

water vapor. The gaseous form of water.

weight. The gravitational force exerted on an object. The name of a good song by *The Band*.

weight density. The weight of an object or substance divided by its volume.

Index

Note: Page numbers in **boldface type** refer to demonstrations.

A

Activities, materials for, xi
Adhesion, 61, 65, **66–67**
Air
    as fluid, 2, 11
    at high altitudes, 94
    push from equator toward poles, 94–95
    rise in low pressure areas, 98
    sink in high pressure areas, 97–98
    speed of heated molecules, 73
    water vapor in, 72
    weight of, 8, **9–10**, 13
    See also Fluids; Gases; Hot air
Air density, **45**
    temperature effect on, **45**, 53–54
    See also Density
Air masses, 87
    continental polar, 90
    continental tropical, 91
    humidity in, 90
    maritime polar, 90–91
    maritime tropical, 91
    molecules above warm vs. cold, 94
Air pressure, 2, 17
    drinking through a straw and, 27, 31
    effect on ears, 4, 5–6
    formula for, 8–9
    gas can functioning and, 32–33
    gas molecules model of, **20–23**
    oxygen removal effect on, **18–19**, 25–26
    at sea level, 10
    temperature effect on, **18–19**, 23–27
    upside-down water glass and card trick, 32, **32**, 65–66
    volume change effect on, **30–31**, 31
    See also Atmospheric pressure; Pressure

Air temperature, polar jet stream and, 96–97
Airplanes
    Bernoulli Effect on wings, 33–35
    jetstream and, 105
    lift of, 34–35
Alcohol, evaporation, 70
Altitude
    air pressure and, 6, 8–9
    increase of air molecules with, 94
Area, pressure and, 3
Atmosphere, 8–9
    extent above Earth, 13
    weight of, **9–10**
Atmospheric pressure, **9–10**, 11, 27
    altitude and, 6, 8–9, 11
    at Earth's surface, 12
    height of atmosphere and, 13
    on the Moon, 31
    at sea level, 9, 10
    See also Air pressure
Average kinetic energy, 74

B
Balloons
    helium, 54
    hot air, 54
The Bends, 12, 43
Bermuda High, 115
Bernoulli Effect, **27–29**, 29–30, **35–36**
    on airplane wings, 33–35
    on moving car with open window, 36–37
    on Ping-Pong ball in funnel, **35–36**, 36
    on toilet flushing, 37
    in tornadoes, 112–113
Buoyancy, 50–51
    of hot air, 53
    measurement of, **45–47**
Buoyant force, 47–52, 53, 55, **55**
    air density effect on, 54
    on boats, **51**, 52
    Cartesian divers, 55, **55**

effect on hot air, 77
fluid displacement effect on, 48, 50, 52, 53
gravity effect on, 51, 52
on submarines, 54

C

Cans, collapsing from pressure, **9–10**
Car windows, Bernoulli Effect and, 36–37
Carbonated beverages, 12
Cartesian divers, 55, **55**
Change of state, 70–71, 80
Cloud seeding, 84
Clouds
   formation of, **78–79**, 79–80, **97**
   in high pressure areas, 97, **97**
   low pressure areas and, 98, 104
   on road surfaces, 85
Cold fronts, 101
   snowfalls and, 102–103
   thunderstorms and, 102
Condensation, 71
   rain and, 80
Condensation nuclei, 79
   cloud seeding and, 84
Conservation of energy, 29
Convection cells, **76–77**, 77, 80–81, 111
   large-scale, 104
   low pressure areas and, 104
   thunderstorms, 111, 116
   tornadoes, 112, 116
Coriolis force, **91**, 92, 103
   hurricanes and, 114, 116
   in northern vs. southern hemisphere, 93, 95, 103
   wind direction and, 95, 98–99
Crowds, motion of, 62–63

D

Dams, water pressure considerations in design, 12
Density, 7, 39, 41, 41–43, 53
   comparison of fluids, **40–41**, **43–44**

of different fluids, **41**, 43, **43**

effects on flotation, **44–45**

fluid displacement and, 109

fluid molecule size and, **44**

impact on temperature of fluids, **45**, 53

mass density, 42

weight density, 42

See also Air density; Water density

Deserts, mountain ranges and, 105

Dew point, 84, 104, 109

E

Eardrums, 5

Ears, pressure sensitivity of, 4, 5–6

Earth

Coriolis force in northern and southern hemispheres, 93, 95, 103

heat absorption, 90

rotation direction, 92–93

sunlight distribution on, **89**, 90, 103, 104

tilt on axis, 89

Energy

heat transfer, 70, 78

for thunderstorms, 71

Energy transfer, in changes of state, 70–71, 80

Equation of continuity, 63–65

Equator

heat absorption at, 90, 103

as low pressure area, 104

sunlight concentration at, **89**, 90, 103, 104

Eustachian tubes, 5

Evaporation, 70, **70**, 111

F

Fluid displacement, 48–50

density effect on, 49

weight of an object and, 49

Fluids, 2, 11

of different densities in contact, **76–77**, 77, 80–81

displacement, density and, 109

equation of continuity, 63–65

speed of, **27–29**, 29–30

viscosity, 65

See also Air; Gases; Liquids

Fog, 84

Force

distribution of, **2–3**, 3, 11

push to areas exerting less force, 23

See also Pressure

Fronts, 101–102, 103

cold, 101, 102

occluded, 101n

precipitation and, 102–103

stationary, 101, 102

warm, 101, 102, 103

G

Gas molecules

model of behavior, **21–23**

movement changes with temperature, 20, **20–23**

space requirements with temperature changes, 20, **20–23**, 23–24

temperature effect on, **18–19**, 19–20, 38

temperature/pressure effects on, 24–25, **24**

Gases, 1, 17

average kinetic energy, 74

change of state from liquid, 70–71

compressibility of, 62

condensation, 71

ideal gas, 20n

kinetic theory of, 20n

temperature, 74

volume, expansion/contraction and, 20, 23–24, 30

See also Air; Gases

Global warming, 115–116

Gravity

hot air and, **76–77**, 77

water pressure and, 7

H

Hailstones, 111–112, 116

Heat
    latent heat of fusion, 71
    latent heat of vaporization, 71
Heat transfer
    from air to person, 73
    evaporation and, 70, **70**
    from person to air, 73
    in substances' change of state, 71
Helium balloons, 54
High pressure areas
    ground temperature and, 97
    polar regions, 104
    scale of, 101
    sinking air in, 97–98
    wind circulation around, 99
Hot air
    buoyancy of, 53
    buoyant force effect on, 77
    density, 45, 77–78, 81
    gravity and, **76–77**, 77
    humidity and, 102
    molecule speed, 73
    rise of, 53, 77–78, 81
    transfer of energy from, 78
    See also Air; Temperature
Hot air balloons, 54
Humidity, 71, 80
    in air masses, 90
    relative humidity, 72, 80
    saturation level and, 71–72, 74
    warm air and, 102
Hurricanes, 116
    conditions needed for, 113–114
    eye of, 114
    loss of strength at landfall, 115, 116
    paths of, 113, 116
Hygrometers, 81, **81–82**

I
Ice, hailstones, 111–112
Ideal gas, 20n

Insects, water striders, 66
Internet, SciLinks, xii

J
Jet streams, 91, 93–97, 105
    airplane flight and, 105
    polar jet stream, 95–97
    seasonal shifts, 97
    storm movement and, 105
    subtropical jet stream, 95–96

K
Kinetic energy, 74
Kinetic theory of gases, 20n, 30

L
Latent heat of fusion, 71
Latent heat of vaporization, 71, 110
Liquids, 1
    change of state from solid, 71, 80
    change of state to gas, 70–71
    drinking through a straw, 27, 31
    how to siphon, **13–15**
    incompressibility of, 62
    speed of heated molecules, **72**, 73
    surface tension, 32, 58–60, **58**, **60**, 65
    See also Fluids
Low pressure areas, 104
    Albuquerque low, 105
    cloud formation and, 79–80
    equatorial region as, 104
    large-scale convection cells and, 104
    rising air in, 98
    scale of, 101
    snow and, 98, 105–106
    wind circulation around, 99, 105–106

M

Magic tricks
   bed of nails, 11–12
   pressure in, 11–12
   upside-down water glass and card, 32, **32**, 65–66
   walking on broken glass, 11, 12
Maps. *See* Weather maps
Mass, concept of, 41–42
Mass density, 42
Measurement units, 3n, 10n
Models, scientific, 21, 30, 65
Moon
   atmospheric pressure, 31
   drinking through a straw on, 31
Mountains
   desert areas and, 105
   effects on storms, 105
   wind updrafts and downdrafts, 82–83

N

Newton's first law, 42

O

Occluded fronts, 101n
Ocean breezes, 75–76, 82
Oceans
   Bermuda High, 115
   fog formation and, 84
   hurricane origins in, 113
Oxidation, **24**, 25, **25–26**
Oxygen, 25

P

Pain levels, force distribution and, 2–3
Paper chromatography, 67
Polar jet stream, 95–96
   air temperature and, 96
   seasonal shifts, 97
Polar molecules, 60–61, 65

Polar regions
    as high-pressure areas, 104
    sunlight at, 90, 103, 104
Prairie dog burrows, 36
Precipitation. *See* Rain; Snow; Storms; Thunderstorms
Pressure, 3, 4, 11
    dam design and, 12
    effect on ears, 5–6
    effect on fluid flow, 5
    effect on human body, 12
    equation for, 3
    force distribution and, 3
    gas pressure, 23
    push from high to low pressure areas, **5**, 7, 11, 23
    use in magic tricks, 11–12
    velocity and, **62**, 63–65, 67
    at water surfaces, 11
    weight and, 7
    See also Air pressure; Force; Water pressure
Pressure areas. *See* High pressure areas; Low pressure areas
Pressure gradient force, 95

R
Rain, 80, 104
    cloud seeding, 84
    condensation role in, 80, 84, 104
    low pressure areas and, 98
    shape of raindrops, 59–60
    See also Thunderstorms
Relative humidity, 72, 80
    air temperature and, 74, 80
    human discomfort and, 82
    indoors, seasonal variation, 83–84
    water vapor and, 72, 80
Roads, mini-clouds on surface of, 85

S
Scientific models, 21, 30, 65
SciLinks, xii
SCUBA diving, 12

Seasons
    jet stream shifts and, 97
    reason for, **88**, 89
    relative humidity changes with, 83–84
Siphons, **13–15**
Smoke particles, 79
Snow
    cold fronts and, 102–103
    condensation role in, 80
    low pressure areas and, 98, 105–106
Soap bubbles, surface tension, 67
Soda pop, 12
Solids, change of state to liquid, 71, 80
Stationary fronts, 101
Storms
    direction of movement, 96
    jet stream influence on, 105
    mountain ranges and, 015
    See also Thunderstorms
Straws, drinking liquid through, 27, 31
Submarines, 54, 55
Subtropical jet stream, 95–96
Sunlight, varied concentrations on Earth, **89**, 90, 103, 104
Super Soakers, **62**, 63–64, 67
Surface tension, 32, 58–60, **58**, **60**, 65
    liquid soap and, 60, 67

T

Temperature, 72
    air density and, **45**, 53–54
    air pressure and, **18–19**, 23–27
    effect on gas molecules, **18–19**, 19–20, 38
    effect on gases, **18–19**, 19–20
    of fluids, density impact on, **45**, 53
    of gases, 74
    in high pressure areas, 97
    molecule speed and, **72**, 73, 80
    rate of change in solids vs. liquids, **72–73**, 74–75
    water density and, **43**, **100**, 102
    See also Hot air
Thunderstorms, **108–109**, 109–111, 116

cold fronts and, 102
convection cells, 111, 116
energy sources, 71
hail formation, 111–112
See also Rain; Storms
Toilet flushing, Bernoulli Effect and, 36–37
Toilets, Bernoulli Effect in flushing, 37
Tornadoes, **108–109**, 112–113, 116
Bernoulli Effect in, 112–113
convection cells, 112, 116
spin direction, 112
Trade winds, 104, 114–115, 116
Transfer of energy. *See* energy transfer

V
Vacuums, siphoning liquids, **13–15**
Viscosity, 65
Volume, 41
Vortexes, 112

W
Warm fronts, 101
Water
adhesion to other substances, 61, **61**, 65, **66–67**
amount in human bodies, 12
dew point, 84, 104, 109
evaporation, 70
as fluid, 2, 11
in human hair, 82
speed in going from large to small cross-sectional area, 63–65
speed of heated molecules, **72**, 73
spin direction in drains, 112
surface tension, 32, 58–60, **58**, **60**, 65
viscosity, 65
Water density, 7–8
freshwater vs. saltwater, 54
temperature effect on, **43**
See also Density
Water molecules
behavior under pressure, 62–63

polarity, 60–61, 65
Water pressure, 2
   dam construction and, 12
   depth and, 6–7
   effects on ears, 6
   equation for, 7–8
   gravity and, 7
   velocity in response to, **62**, 63–65
   See also pressure
Water strider (insect), 66
Water temperature, density and, **100**, 102
Water vapor, 23–24
   cloud seeding and, 84
   condensation, 71, 84, 104, 114n
   condensation nuclei and, 79
   effect on pressure, 23–27
   in hot vs. cold air, 72, 74, 80
   latent heat, 71, 110
   relative humidity and, 72, 80
   saturation level, 71–72, 74
Weather, on local scale, 69
Weather maps, symbols, 97, 101
Weight
   of air, **9–10**
   gravity and, 7
   of objects in water, 47
   pressure and, 7
Weight density, 42
Wind
   circulation around high pressure areas, 99
   circulation around low pressure areas, 99, 105–106
   direction
      changes in, 100
      Coriolis force and, 95, 98–99
      at high-altitude, 95
   in hurricanes, 114–115, 116
   local winds, 75–76, 82–83
   on mountainsides, 82–83
   ocean breezes, 75–76, 82
   speed at high altitude, 95
   trade winds, 104, 114–115, 116

National Science Teachers Association